THE FUTURE: CREATING TOMORROW'S SOCCER PLAYERS TODAY

9 KEY PRINCIPLES FOR COACHES FROM SPORT PSYCHOLOGY

TOM BATES

DARK RIVER

An imprint of Bennion Kearny Ltd.

Published in 2017 by Dark River, an imprint of Bennion Kearny Limited.

Copyright © Dark River

ISBN: 978-1-911121-43-5

Published by Dark River, Bennion Kearny Limited
6 Woodside
Churnet View Road
Oakamoor
Staffordshire
ST10 3AE

www.BennionKearny.com

Dedicated to my Grandfather, Frederick Charles Bates. A man who lived a remarkable life and taught me about the true depth of human potential. I can understand why God wanted you close to him.

ACKNOWLEDGEMENTS

It has been a sincere privilege to share some of the lessons I have encountered over the last 12 years of my career in this book. To quote Sir Isaac Newton, "If I have seen further than most it is because I have been standing on the shoulders of giants." This book wouldn't have been possible without the many great teachers I have been blessed to have had in the short course of my early career.

To my Mother and Father – Clive and Sandra Bates – my first outstanding coaches who supported, empowered, and fed my enthusiasm: "Your best will always be good enough for us." To my amazing wife Hannah and her leading example for our three children – Josiah, Isabelle, and Noah – which helps them to flourish every day. You are the most important team of all – I love you. Thank you to Bill and Val Beswick, my long-term friends, mentors, and colleagues, without whom I would not be where I am today. To my good friend Joe Roach who allowed me my first chance to coach in the professional game all those years ago. To Lee Carsley who encouraged, inspired, and believed. To Ruben Bonastre and FC Barcelona for teaching me virtues beyond the ball. To Steve Round and Dan Ashworth, both innovative visionary directors who have taught, guided, and provided the leading light. To Mike Scott, who drilled me into shape; turning a disorganised idealist into a functional practitioner to pass my A licence and for all the hours crammed into the minibus travelling up and down the country. To John Downes, who is a true force of endless energy, and a creative mastermind. Publishers Bennion Kearny for the support, guidance, and direction with this first release. To Ray Power for his time and commitment. I am privileged to have had the opportunity to be taught by some outstanding men and women and this book is dedicated to them all.

Finally to the players – the real teachers – who over the years have taught me the true meaning of what it is to be called 'coach'.

Almost every successful person begins with two beliefs:
The Future can be better than the present
and I have the power to make it so.

David Brooks

FOREWORD

As the evolution of coaching practice continues to advance, the importance of applied sport psychology will play a central role in that movement. Having worked as assistant manager and first team coach at Everton and Manchester United in the English Premier League, I know the power and impact that creating positive winning attitudes within a team can have. Much of my own work as a coach at the very highest level, including the progressive time spent with the senior England national team was underpinned by a drive to learn. As a coach, my own pursuit of constant improvement was at the heart of my work.

As Director of Football at Aston Villa FC, I place a high value on Tom's experience and ideas. He possesses the unique combination of visionary insight and practical knowledge of the game. Tom's journey as a young coach, gaining his UEFA A licence then qualifying in psychology has enabled him to operate ahead of the game. Together, we are working creatively to build a coaching environment that embraces tradition, whilst thinking forwards into the future. Tom's work with players and coaches will continue to be an essential ingredient for the sustained success of a team and club culture striving to achieve competitive excellence.

Coaches and players who understand the importance of a positive mentality to achieve competitive toughness is paramount at all levels of the game. Developing a winning mindset through fostering healthy relationships will become a defining skill for the coach of the future. Tom is without doubt a leading practitioner in his field and this book is a rare blend of inspiration and simple actionable strategy for coaches at all levels of the game"

Steve Round, Director of Football, Aston Villa FC

TABLE OF CONTENTS

INTRODUCTION 1

PRINCIPLE 1: THE RELATIONSHIP COACH................................. 3

    The Winning Mind and The Relationship Coach................................ 4

    Inside Out Coaching 7

    The Human Being 8

    What are Leadership and Management? 8

    Specific actions.. 12

        Open the door 12

        One-to-one player meeting.. 12

        Share something of yourself.. 12

        Co-create the goal 12

        The Player Profile... 12

        The Performance Profile... 13

        Understand the Barriers 14

        Personal De-Brief / Effective Intervention................................ 15

    Summary 15

PRINCIPLE 2 UNDERSTAND THE JOB YOU HAVE BEEN
BROUGHT IN TO DO 17

    Specific actions.. 22

    Exercises.. 23

    Recruitment, Evaluation and Analysis.. 23

    Relationships.. 24

    Mission and Purpose.. 25

        Story 25

        Character Counts.. 25

        Assessing Character.. 26

        Understanding Self, Understanding the Situation...................... 26

Summary 27

PRINCIPLE 3: BUILDING A POSITIVE ATTITUDE 29

Michael Jordan 29

Attitude Drives Performance 30

Beckham's Brilliance 32

Kirsty's Mind Gym Exercises – 6 keys that led to positive change. 34

Specific actions 35

From Negative to Positive 36

Summary 39

PRINCIPLE 4: A LEADER'S LANDSCAPE 41

Clarity - The Catalyst for Confidence 41

The Power of Three 43

Use of Questions 43

Pictures paint a thousand words 44

The Separation of Performance from Identity 44

Gareth Southgate – A New England Culture for the Three Lions. 45

Specific actions 46

Set standards 47

Summary 48

PRINCIPLE 5: CONFIDENCE AND CULTURE 49

What is a 'Fear of Failure'? 49

Choice in Challenge 51

Ingredients of a Response-*ABLE* Mindset 53

Grit 53

Growth 54

Confidence 55

Self-Worth 59

Developing a Response-*ABLE* Mindset 59

The 'secret' to Lionel Messi's Success 59

Re-Defining Success (and Failure).. 60

Create Certainty through Training.. 63

Controlling the Controllables... 64

Exercises.. 64

Creating a Culture Code... 64

Shared Ownership – A Natural Way to Create Accountability ... 65

Specific actions... 65

Define Success.. 65

Re-define failure 66

Share Your Story 66

Instil Confidence.. 66

Summary 66

PRINCIPLE 6: ESTABLISH ACCOUNTABILITY 67

Time Travel - The Cost of Ambition 67

The past is for learning from, not living in................................. 69

Specific actions.. 72

Create a Player-Led Individual Athletic Development Plan 72

The Drive to Succeed.. 75

The Response-Able Mindset.. 76

Fighting Fit.. 77

Constant and Never-ending Improvement................................ 79

Rewarding Attitude over Ability – A Coach's Imperative............ 80

Specific actions for establishing accountability................................. 81

Summary 81

PRINCIPLE 7: EXPLAIN YOUR STYLE OF PLAY 83

What is a Style of Play?.. 83

Style of play example 84

Specific Actions... 84

Style of Play – Six Key Questions 84

Communication in Coaching 84

Sir Clive Woodward 85

Specific actions 87

    Ask the 'Right' Questions 88

    Saying nothing is sometimes best 88

    Bite-sized is best 89

    Everyone's different 89

    Communicate to alleviate 89

Specific actions 90

Summary 91

PRINCIPLE 8: 80:20 93

No Limit Thinking 94

Jack Butland's No Limit Thinking 94

The Why Not Voice Within 95

    Supreme Confidence 95

    Honing Jack's No Limit Thinking 96

Champion Coaches and Players are No Limit Thinkers 97

    Performing to Expectations 98

Muhammad Ali's Self-Belief: Power of the Inner Voice 100

We Create the Good Days and the Bad 101

The Science behind Visualisation 102

The Biology of Self-Belief 105

No Limits Thinking Comes With Doing What Makes
You Happy 105

The Power of Optimism - Opportunities not Limits 106

Helping Players Train the Brain 107

Specific actions 108

Exercises 109

Summary 111

PRINCIPLE 9: MANAGING SELF...113

   Cool and Calm Breeds Clear and Confident........................113

      5 Questions for Coaches on Matchday:.........................114

   Specific Actions...115

   Usain Bolt – Knowing Self...115

   Managing My State 116

   Inner Dialogue or Self-Talk 117

      Frame thoughts...119

      Know the script...119

      Practice makes progress 119

   Physiology and Body Language....................................119

      Modelling positive empowering body language yourself...........120

      Tell, See, Do..120

      Role Model Memory...120

      Try it on...120

   Breathing...121

   Exercises...121

      The Mind Sweep..122

   A coach's final message 122

   The Pre-Performance Routine......................................123

   Image and Appearance..125

   'How do we become successful?' - The 10 Key Components.......126

   Specific actions: During the match................................127

   Half-Time...128

   Specific Actions...129

Summary...130

WARRIORS NEVER GIVE UP...131

EPILOGUE...133

INTRODUCTION

From the earliest age, I can remember running, jumping, and climbing; being physically active, engaged in sport, and playing games was a big part of my childhood. I fell in love with the thrill of competing and pushing personal physical boundaries. There were two simple things I loved about sport: 1. I loved the challenge, and 2. I loved the opportunity to constantly improve with practice.

My footballing career at Cambridge United FC ended in 'failure', but I went on to study Sports Psychology at university. I've been privileged as a player to have experienced the rollercoaster of ambition and disappointment, hope and loss. I know the familiarity of triumph, and I've felt the heartache of defeat, both as a player and as a coach. And it's here that you will find the perspective of this book.

There are no secrets to success, but there are fundamental principles that underpin successful teams and individuals. Psychology has a huge part to play in that success, and this book captures the simplicity and application of that work in action from elite sport and business.

This book is a reflection of the remarkable lessons I've been sincerely privileged to share with so many elite performers in my early career within professional sport. By offering some key advice, and inviting you to use the methods and models within this book, it is my genuine wish that I assist you on your coaching journey. The lessons you encounter within this book are a result of years of applied experience within elite sport and personal development coaching. I am honoured to be able to share these lessons with you in the hope that you will use them to positively influence your players, and teams, and the lives they go on to live.

In this book, I will share some of the most recent performance-enhancing techniques for you to use, apply, and improve your own coaching practice. The book will inspire, energise, and challenge you to think in new ways, search for more sustainable solutions to the challenges you face, and provide personal guidance to create better results in all areas of work as a coach.

It has been widely documented in the Sports Psychology literature that thinking styles, thoughts, and thought patterns significantly impact the emotions of elite sport performers. In both scientific research and applied elite performance domains there is a commonly held belief that attaining and sustaining an appropriate emotional state is central to success, and the last decade has witnessed exciting advances in cognitive and emotional regulation research.

This book offers insights for coaches on the integration of practically applied coaching strategies for improving players' mindsets. It is an opportunity to study techniques based on the science of psychology that will help improve the mental and emotional traits required to succeed.

I've been entrusted to work alongside and explore how the power of a positive, healthy mental attitude can act to support, assist, and guide others to grow, develop, and improve. I've learned how to help athletes, coaches, teams, organisations and business leaders get the best from themselves and each other whilst facing some of the toughest challenges on and off their respective fields of play. I'm delighted for the first time to be able to share with you some of my most cherished experiences with high achievers in a variety of disciplines and invite you to put these ideas into action to improve your coaching practice. It is a testament to the people who have agreed to feature in this book – their openness and willingness to share – that we have this great opportunity to learn – whoever you are, and wherever you may be on your own coaching journey.

> **What you get, give. What you learn, teach.**
> **It will take you all over the world.**
>
> Maya Angelou

Wishing you every success!

Tom

PRINCIPLE 1
THE RELATIONSHIP COACH

> I've learned that people will forget what you said, they will forget what you did, but they will never forget how you made them feel.
>
> Maya Angelou

Seeing the world through the eyes of your players is fundamental if you want to get the very best from them. Each player is unique, with a different profile, personality, and purpose. True empathy unlocks your ability to relate to their tensions, anxieties, frustrations, and ambitions. When you understand the person, you get double from the player. We are human beings; we all feel the need to be valued and loved, to contribute, and to feel connected.

*

This book was written from the perspective of attempting to understand the practical experiences of coaches. It was written so that they may apply the principles within it to improve their coaching and themselves.

There are two fundamental truths at the heart of effective modern day and future coaching – leadership and management – and, of these, the very best coaches think *forward*. To stay ahead of the game, they operate in the present, but they think in the future. What worked yesterday won't work today. What works today will not work in the future. Here's why.

- Yesterday, hierarchy was the model; today, successful teams are bred on equality.
- Yesterday's leaders commanded the ship; today's facilitate their crew's synergy.
- Yesterday's managers demanded respect; today's encourage self-respect.
- Yesterday's employees waited for orders; today's teams innovate.
- Yesterday's senior status signified superiority; today, collaboration is king.
- Yesterday, results drove value; today, your core values drive the results.

- Yesterday's leaders commanded control. Tomorrow's leaders must inspire and empower.

And nowhere do you see these things more than when working with your players.

Let's explore this in more detail.

Dictatorial leadership is dying. High-performance engagement and training in the modern football world is based on effective negotiation underpinned by an appreciation for human personality and motivational values.

The coach of the future is not an X's and O's strategist (though this is, of course, a non-negotiable foundation), they are a developer of people, and will require an unparalleled knowledge and appreciation for the nature of human development. This is true for coaches working with players at all levels of the game, from the grassroots community and academy to the senior professional and international stage.

The stupid footballer is dead. The availability of information through the internet means that players (like people) don't blindly follow anyone, anywhere, anymore. They learn and gain knowledge independently. Accordingly, the leaders who only know how to dictate will die.

The Winning Mind and The Relationship Coach

The future coach is a coach who recognises the importance of building psychological confidence through task clarity and emotional connection. Creating effective winning relationships with players is, as research teaches us, a unique blend of affection and authority.

> **People don't care how much you know until they know how much you care.**
>
> Theodore Roosevelt

In 2009, educational research from professors Judy Dunn and Richard Layard presented some key findings associated with creating effective learning environments. They surveyed more than 25,000 children from schools in the UK, in order to address the question "*What makes the most effective teaching style?*"

Ultimately, they found two factors that defined the effectiveness of each teacher. The first they labelled *control*, a characteristic that reflected the ability of the teacher to maintain order and task progression within the learning environment (e.g., keeping students' behaviour in-check and on task). The second was *warmth*. This quality reflected the level of affection and positive energy the teachers elicited whilst teaching, typified by inter- and intra-personal qualities and characteristics.

From these two factors, four main teaching styles were categorised and rated for their corresponding effectiveness within the learning environment. The first style was labelled as *Militant*. This type of teacher has complete control in the environment, dictating with precision and power. Students corresponded with compliance and clear non-negotiables in terms of behaviour were established and corrected immediately. High in control, but low in warmth, this type of teaching style was effective but not found to be optimal. Although task compliance was very high, students did not always feel they could ask questions relating to the task as they felt afraid or nervous about asking a 'stupid question' or feeling negatively judged by their teacher.

The second teaching style highlighted was *Neglectful*. This type of teacher – low in *control* and low in *warmth* – created an unstructured learning environment in which the students did not feel cared for.

The third teaching style identified in this ground-breaking educational research was labelled as *Permissive*. Typified by high levels of *warmth*, students loved having fun in the classroom, but whenever the teacher needed to take control or move the lesson forward, they struggled. Locked in a perilous fight to shape the structure of the lesson, students became unruly and unfocused.

The fourth and final teaching style that was identified, unequivocally, as the most effective was labelled *authoritative*. Layard and Dunn found that the central components of an effective learning environment was one where the teacher had complete *control* with a clear demonstration of *warmth*. Students knew what they had to do and also felt cared for enough to ask questions, make mistakes, and be secure with the teacher's trust. An *authoritative* teacher has sound subject knowledge and understanding backed up by a range of human relationship skills which builds emotional connection and psychological confidence.

The Control Warmth Matrix

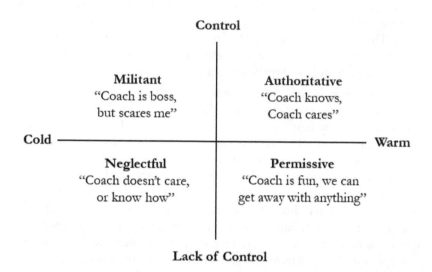

When considering these fundamental teaching/leadership qualities, and the influence they elicit in the classroom learning environment, it becomes apparent that we can apply them in coaching. After all, great coaches are great teachers.

> **Educating the mind without educating the heart is no education at all.**
> Aristotle

A coach's great privilege is to realise that they are more than the tactics, strategies, and systems they create to execute a winning game plan, although these are, of course, paramount. In recognising the importance of building healthy positive relationships to create winning attitudes, coaches gain the opportunity to become much more than an expert in strategy. They gain a capacity to enrich the hearts and minds of their players, assisting them in transforming previous levels of performance. They foster the mental, emotional, and social qualities required to create the winning player and – more importantly – person of the future.

Inside Out Coaching

In his brilliant and profound book *Inside Out Coaching – How Sports Can Transform Lives*, author Joe Ehrmann, an ex-All-American and NFL championship defensive lineman, articulates the difference between two kinds of coaches: transactional and transformational.

According to Joe, most coaches fail to recognise the true power of their platform to help, teach, coach, and inspire their athletes to live happier more empowered lives. This type of coach is transactional. This type of coach uses their players as a ticket to validate their own personal needs of self-importance, status, and identity. A transactional coach uses their power and influence to manipulate players in order to exert dominance, driven by an unfulfilled need to feel superior. Whilst this type of coach can sometimes be successful in terms of competitive outcomes, their achievements are often short-lived and unsustainable, normally due to an inability to get out of the way of their own egos as well as failures in nurturing human relationships.

I remember a coach at a professional academy who was known for 'over-coaching'. Each 90-minute session was taken up with countless coach interventions and mini-lectures. At each staff event, this coach took the time to persuade other coaches that he was the reason for a specific win or a player's improvement. One evening, the Academy manager decided to make some coach observations and offer some constructive feedback. Having watched the coach in question, he noted that the players were stood still for 57 minutes out of the 90. The Academy manager handed the coach his feedback form with the following phrase underlined in bold: "Remember who you're there for." Later, he explained to him that coaches who coach for themselves end up losing their players.

The transformational coach, by comparison, uses their platform to unleash the power and potential of their players by appealing to their sense of self-worth and value to the world. Transformational coaches possess the ability to place their players' needs above their own, becoming what Joe calls *'Inside Out Coaches'*. Operating from a drive to create empathy, connection, and guidance, inside out coaches work to build a sense of inner purpose, value, and inner self-worth in their players. Joe offers the following tips on how to become a *transformational* coach:

- Put yourself in your players' shoes and ask what they need first.
- Reflect back on your own experiences of success and failure and ask how these experiences have had an impact on you as a coach.

- Place your players' needs above your own.
- Recognise the power of your influence as a role model to positively shape a young person's life, forever.
- Ask yourself these questions:
    - *Why* do I coach?
    - *How* does it feel to be coached by me?
    - *Why* do I coach the way I coach?

Coaches who understand their own world, and who can make sense of their lives, maximise their chances to impact the lives of the young people around them positively. Tracing back the unfulfilled needs they have as athletes gives them the best opportunity to transcend their own search for personal validation through their players. Unshackled from their own insecurity, an inside out coach infuses the spirit of inspiration and love that goes far beyond winning and losing.

The Human Being

Successful high-performance cultures and environments are based on the effective art of negotiation and an understanding of human needs. Every player has become a brand in their own right at the highest level. The future player will be like managing a limited company, and an appreciation of individual needs will be critical. Technology and financial freedom brings an independence of thought in society and understanding the human elements of each person in the team (to maximise their potential and 'talent') will be paramount. Team aims and objectives must be central but connected to the personal agendas of each player.

What are Leadership and Management?

> **Only by knowing yourself can you become an effective leader.**
> Vince Lombardi

There are many different interpretations of leadership and management. It has been suggested that "Management is more about *what* and Leadership is more concerned with *how* you do." Mark Proctor.

Without a doubt, the great coaches of the past have taught us over and over again that only through knowing yourself, and having a solid understanding of your own personal values, can you develop character and integrity. Through *being* the example, a true leader unconsciously transfers their character and signposts their integrity.

The effective leader creates the right environment for the best behaviours to occur and evolve based on their key values. This is important when we think about the implications and changes required to meet the identified future needs of the coach's changing leadership, and management landscape.

> **Advances in information technology, communication and multi-cultural diversity create for a world that is faster and more connected than ever before. Consequently, we must become familiar with these changes if we are to capitalise on our future.**
>
> Jeanne Brett, Kristin Behfar and Mary Kern

So, what does the future look like? What traits must the successful future leader have?

> **Telecommunications progressed from telegraph to telephone, from copper wires to fiber-optics, from analog to digital, from wireless to satellite. I believe the industry will change more in the next five to 10 years than it has in the last 50.**
>
> Mary Barra, Chairman and CEO of GM

The future will be faster, and people will be able to gather information from multiple sources rapidly. By 2025, it is predicted that 95% of children from eight years of age, and above, will have their own handheld telecommunications device. This will influence modes of communication and coaching strategies and change the very nature of social interaction.

Leaders of the future will need to empower players to self-manage and become better equipped at facilitative capabilities. The new era of tomorrow's coaching world will require coaches to foster and support creative independence. Independence of thought, decision making, and action. The new successful performance culture of the future will witness a power shift from coach-led player support, to player-led coach support.

PRINCIPLE 1

The successful coach of the future will:

1. Understand and integrate technology to engage, stimulate, and retain attention.
2. Create deep and meaningful relationships with players based on authentic trust.
3. Facilitate coaching practice by creating independent, co-created decision-making opportunities.

The future coach must possess an ability to learn fast and apply knowledge from multiple sources. They must have a strong sense of leadership but retain an openness for new knowledge and be prepared at any moment to change in favour of an improved way of working. Above all else, they must be mindful of the multi-disciplinary nature of high performance and consider themselves both a master and a student in the same breath.

Leadership and management are about knowing yourself inside out. Although times change, the principles of success don't. Being unselfish, curious, hardworking and humble are admirable qualities that have caused me to engage with, and follow, the leaders who have guided my own career. As well as sticking to these principles, we must always question the norm to find new ways of doing things better. We must keep wanting to improve, all the time.

The future coach must be able to work across multiple disciplines, and become a reader and enthusiast for the expertise that enables learning, growth, and improvement. Technological advances will mean that the future high-performance environment will be data rich. Analysis of that data and intelligent selection will play a huge role in creating and sustaining a successful culture and environment.

We already live in a world where we receive things instantaneously. The way we communicate via our handheld devices allows us to send and receive information straightaway. That changes the way people think, act and behave. The support resources surrounding the players now are on the verge of being overwhelming. We are in danger of being the most over-resourced yet under-resourceful generation. The leader of the future will need to be an outstanding *curator* of the many resources available to maximise potential, efficiency, and development – both at staff and player levels.

> **We live in an age of instant gratification and that is only going to get faster. We must evolve with the modern modes of communication but retain the stoic moral values of our heritage and tradition.**
>
> Dan Ashworth, Director of Elite Development,
> The English Football Association

Effectively utilizing the abundance of resources at a technological, data, and staffing level requires a clear and prioritized understanding of your players' immediate, short- and long-term needs. For instance, the endless match analysis data presented pre, during, and after a match can swamp any player. Knowing what you want to measure, when, and why, is as important as how much of it is delivered.

Arsène Wenger, Manager of Arsenal FC, is well known for his beliefs about a coach's ability to deliver concise information at the right times. For example, at half-time he will only focus on three points in possession and three points when out of possession so as to avoid information overload. He does this to appeal to the players' needs in the context of the situation.

Knowing his players, the emotions at that time, and the short window to communicate key messages, Wenger is able to adapt his management style to cater to his players' needs. As a coach, he has selected key information presented by his analysts, digested it himself, and publically communicated the relevant messages to the team in a language and tone that fits the context and the culture.

Whilst a coach communicates with his team publically, they are also aware that connecting with individuals before and afterwards can be as valuable as the group message. Some players need a quiet one-to-one to clarify information and boost confidence, others need to be left alone to self-manage. Some need a kick up the backside, and others require a pat on the back. What's most important here is that, as the coach, you have a very good understanding about what works for each of them. This understanding is only gained through time, patience, and the creation of opportunities for constant communication.

PRINCIPLE 1

Specific actions

A central theme running through this book is empathy and understanding. As a coach, see the world through the eyes of your players. Understand the challenges each player is facing. We will re-visit a multitude of exercises, similar in nature, to emphasise and reinforce alternative methods of achieving particular traits and underlining their importance for coaches as a cornerstone in their players' development.

Open the door

Every player needs to know that there is always an opportunity (should they need it) to come and speak with their coach. When players are young, this also goes for parents. Reassurance is like medicine and sometimes just knowing the door is open provides a sense of security and connection.

One-to-one player meeting

Create an opportunity to invite a player to meet with you privately.

Take the time to get to know something about them that you didn't know before. This could be where they live or where they were born, which team they support, or their favourite player in the world. The simpler the better.

Share something of yourself

Effective relationships are built on trust. Make sure the player leaves you having learned something about you too. This will ensure that they feel they know you a little better. This could be a favourite musician, food, or family fact.

Co-create the goal

Know your players' ambitions and motivations to achieve their goals. This is the essence of seeing the world through their eyes. Create development goals *together* rather than imposing them.

The Player Profile

Take the time to build a performance profile in which the technical, tactical, physical, and mental traits required to succeed are logged. These traits should be the ones the player (and you as coach) believe are needed to be the very best in their position. This will help you build the player's job description and offer a vital tool for measurement and accountability.

Ensure that the player takes ownership (under your guidance) to list their traits and set their goals.

For example, a striker may label:

- Physical: Strength to hold defenders off, Acceleration to break away from defenders.
- Technical: Close range finishing one-on-one.
- Tactical: How to play as a 'false 9' in a 4-3-3.
- Mental: Staying confident after missing key opportunities.
- Emotional: Staying calm and composed in 1 v1 situations.
- Social: Speak at the team meeting and offer opinions.
- Personal: Create time for my family, call mum and dad once a week!
- Lifestyle: Ensure I'm in bed before 11 pm each night. Replace nutritional plan every week.

The Performance Profile

The player performance profile is a tool to measure, manage, and monitor specific traits required to succeed in each position. It is a collaborative method for facilitating performance development and improvement.

The profile can be used to both write and record performance goals in each category, and track progress over time. There is an sample blank profile, below.

Under the category of "Emotional", for example, the coach and player can assess player components such as:

- The ability to stay composed under pressure.
- Energy to motivate himself/herself.
- Remaining calm in conflict.

When making an assessment:

1. Coaches ask their player: "Where do you think you are now, between 0 and 10?"
2. Coaches then offer their own assessment of the player: "This is where I think you are."

3. Both parties examine the differences between scores/viewpoints.
4. Both parties try to work out why there are differences in perceptions.
5. The coach and player then calculate a score, and work out what can be done to improve the score, for this player, in this situation.

The current score – between 0 and 10 – is then marked on the profile wheel (0 = low grade, 10 = high grade; 10 is the outermost ring).

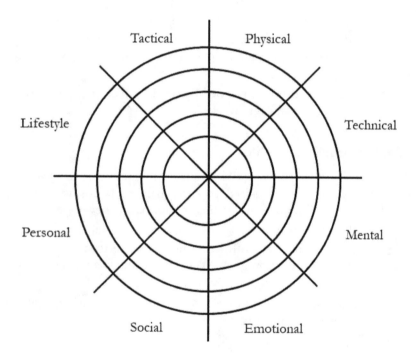

Understand the Barriers

When you understand the things that can get in the way of a player achieving their goals, you can effectively help to remove them. For example, travel to training in the evening may be a problem due to lack of transport options. Providing transport removes the anxiety associated with the problem and creates more time to focus on the goal of constant improvement.

Personal De-Brief / Effective Intervention

During a de-brief, make a short list of the player's strengths and areas for improvement. If you have access to the stats on their performances, or video clips, they are excellent tools. Sandwich the feedback, presenting a key strength, then an area for improvement, followed by another strength. This structure reassures the player that there were good things in the performance and that there are also areas to improve on. Crucially, end any interaction on a positive note!

Summary

What worked yesterday won't work today and what works today won't work tomorrow. The future coach will continue to innovate, recognising and adapting to the constant developments in technology and society which are changing the way we live and engage with the world around us.

The way information is shared and taught in educational institutions will rapidly be aided by an emerging trend of virtual online advancements.

Despite the rise and benefit of information technology, and the need to incorporate teaching methods accordingly, the future coach *must* appeal to the connection and relationship with the human being. Inevitably, relationships will be defined in an age of independence by a coach's capacity to see the world through the eyes of their players, placing players' needs above their own.

The future coach must work toward sustaining high-performance environments that allow for co-created independent thinking, both on the pitch and off it. Modern-day winning cultures will evolve to allow constant interchange between player-led coach-supported, and coach-led player-supported, working dynamics. The future coach will need to be an architect of *affectionate authority* riding the crest of innovation whilst remaining grounded in the foundation of their core values. In an age when dictatorships will continue to fall, collaboration will be crowned the new king, and the future coach will rise.

PRINCIPLE 2
UNDERSTAND THE JOB
YOU HAVE BEEN BROUGHT
IN TO DO

> **Seek first to understand and then to be understood.**
>
> St Francis of Assisi

Every club and team has different objectives; for some, it is to win the league, for others to avoid the drop. Senior environments are largely driven and defined by results, whereas holistic development programmes form more of a priority in youth development settings.

At all levels of the game, from amateur to professional, understanding your job and how it fits into your club's overall vision, culture and philosophy is crucial.

In this principle, we look to fully understand (from the perspectives of owners, senior coaches, parents – whomever the stakeholders are) the job you have been brought in to do.

*

In 2011, I was fortunate to spend some time studying and learning at one of the greatest football clubs in the world: FC Barcelona.

For a long time, I had watched from afar, admiring the beauty, class, and innovation of the club; a club that played a style of football which entertained and captured the hearts of millions of football supporters around the world. Barcelona weren't just winning, they were making the world fall in love with the way they were winning.

When my visit came together, I touched down in Barcelona and my head was racing. What will I ask? What are the most important questions? What do I really want to learn? Are my clothes smart and respectful enough? I wonder if I can take pictures to capture the magic and wisdom I encounter?

My mind ran overtime about every little detail, but in those few days, I was completely alive. I didn't need an alarm clock – my excitement woke me in the morning and kept me awake late into the evening. Anyone that knows this feeling realises, at heart, where their passion truly lies.

In the stillness of the night before my training ground visit, my thoughts settled as I re-evaluated the intention of my exploration. I wanted to know one thing: the inspired ingredients of their greatness recipe.

It was only after the trip that I realised there were no secrets, but there were clearly upheld principles, which the club – in its typical spirit of openness – was happy to share.

I knew I had a duty to share some of the most cherished lessons I'd learned. I felt coaches everywhere needed to know this stuff. So on the final evening, following a dinner at the Nou Camp, I grabbed my notepad and began gathering my thoughts in reflection.

Here's what I learned.

1. Uphold the culture

Upon arrival, each member of staff from the first team manager to the U7's coach meets, and is greeted by, the President of the club, Josep Maria Bartomeu, with a very important message, "The main priority of your position is to uphold the spirit and culture of this club, because the spirit and culture of the club will be here long after we are gone."

2. Respect in action

Before training each evening, every age group greets their teammates' parents and families with handshakes and hugs before practice. When equipment is moved, every player works to move it. Not a single player is left out of moving the goals for the match, in every age group within the academy, from the U7's all the way to the U18's. Before competitive matches, the opposition are honoured with team applause with the hosts finally forming a huddle to prepare for kick off.

3. Cool and calm breeds clear and confident

During the U18 FCB versus Bayer Leverkusen match, the German coach bounded up and down the touchline with a clipboard and whistle barking orders to his players. Each one of Barcelona's coaches sat calmly in the shade of the dugout allowing the players to think independently, breed self-reliance, and solve the problems in the storm of the game together. No destructive criticism, no stressful reactions, no negative input.

The game was physically tough and finished 1-1, but one team earned a great deal more than a point in the match. When I asked the FC Barcelona coach why he did not intervene and coach the players during difficult times, he smiled, and simply said, "If we coach the players during match day, how will we ever get to understand how much they know? Matchday is their opportunity to demonstrate their learning from the week and show us, independently of us, how much they know. The result is never the most important outcome. The demonstration of learning is most important for us."

4. Champions set their own standards – the body follows the mind

After the Champions League quarter-final against Arsenal in 2011, I watched the first team training the next day. They trained for 45 minutes at a very high intensity. Explosive sprints combined with ball work and short, sharp agility runs around poles. Punch passes zipped off the surface with speed and tenacity under the direction of head coach Pep Guardiola.

This was no cool down session.

The previous night's game had been a tough encounter with Barcelona winning 3-1 at Camp Nou. When I asked the coach why they were training so hard, he simply said, "We believe the body follows what the mind tells it to do. It's our way." It was then that it struck me. This is why *this team* is one of the best in the world. They are prepared to do what no-one else is, to reach levels no-one else can.

5. Labour of love

Each member of staff from the cleaner to the cook and coach is reminded of the purpose of their role within the training ground. Regular meetings are held with all staff, irrespective of role or duty, and messages are passed on from the President. The last meeting's message was a simple one, "My job and your job is a labour of love; if it is not, we will fail."

6. Humility

The president of the club has his HQ on the ground floor of the public ice rink in Camp Nou. Each day, he eats in the public canteen. No matter whether you're the cleaner or the driver of the team coach, the President allows anyone to sit with him over lunch. His accessible presence in the public canteen demonstrates the equality of culture at the club. He knows that in his extraordinary position, his main job is to represent the Catalan people with humility.

7. Togetherness

At lunch one day, I was pointed in the direction of a 10-year-old Japanese boy who the club had just recruited. On his table were the reserve team coach Luis Enrique, the U18 Captain, and a mixture of academy players and first team players. I was struck by how the young boy was completely at home in the presence of the other club members. During the lunch, Enrique poured water into the glasses of the players, and laughter broke out in a totally relaxed atmosphere. It was clear that this was a family. The first team are connected to their roots – "This is where we came from" – and the Academy are inspired to learn and be together.

8. Mes que en club – "More than a club"

Founded in 1899 by Joan Gamper, FC Barcelona have been pivotal in the defence of Catalan interests, and persecution from Spain's dictatorship in the 20th century. Propelled by this social and moral honour to defend Catalanism, the club actively supports and promotes cultural virtues around the world, aligning their mission to the phrase, "beyond what belongs in the realm of sport."

The FCB Foundation operates across 41 different countries around the world. Its virtues such as charity, humility, honesty, and respect underpin a strong moral philosophy helping some of the poorest communities to grow and develop using sport and the brand of FC Barcelona. Unlike other football clubs around the world, the fans own FC Barcelona. In a democratic election, the fans vote for the president to represent their club, which is a symbol for the Catalan culture. The club now has teams represented in roller hockey, basketball, rugby, and futsal.

9. Person first, then player

The education programme for all players is considered as important as football development. The club believes in creating well-rounded, thinking players who display wisdom. At the time of my visit, Xavi, Iniesta and five other first-team players (as well as nine Reserve team players) were studying for degrees alongside their football careers. As soon as Cesc Fabregas signed back to FCB from Arsenal, in 2011, he called his old teacher (whom he had not seen for five years) to request his attendance at the homecoming party personally.

10. The Football Family

At the start of the 2011 season, the first team manager requested that the local television company (TV3) create a film of Eric Abidal to be played before the next home match. The manager instructed them not to include footage of goals or frills, but of the hard tackles he had won, the running he did, and the challenges he had faced in games. The final clip was to be Abidal on his knees praying in the hospital and then fade out. At this time, Eric Abidal was fighting a battle with cancer. The film was played to the first team at Camp Nou, the entire Academy, and every member of staff to remind them of their connection to one another.

*

Of course, many clubs won't have as far-reaching a philosophy as Barcelona. But it is important that you get a clear brief when you take over as a coach; a brief that details what your club's values, beliefs, and expectations are.

Knowing this will give you a greater understanding of your context and help you succeed in your role. Here's one idea I shared with a men's senior first-team coach in England. Our session together was simple and focused on three main themes: *mission, purpose,* and *direction*. Firstly, it is important to distinguish between the three terms. Although varying definitions exist we defined them in the session as follows:

- **Mission** – *What* we are trying to achieve
- **Purpose** – *Why* we are trying to achieve it
- **Direction** – *Where* we want to go and *how* we are going to get there

After sharing some ideas in discussion together, the head coach defined his mission, purpose, and direction very clearly and very simply.

- **Mission** – Creating a successful club that people (*staff and players*) feel connected to; a club they care about and work hard for.
- **Purpose** – I believe that doing the right thing, living with integrity, and working hard will create long-term success (Premier League Status).
- **Direction** – (*Where*) To be promoted to the Premier League through (*How*) being brave enough to think differently, and recruiting hungry people who are driven to learn, practice, and improve.

In the space below, think about or write down what the mission, purpose, and direction will be for your team.

PRINCIPLE 2

MISSION	PURPOSE	DIRECTION
The thing I want to achieve	Why I am going to achieve it	Where I want to go, and how to get there

Let's take a moment to look at particular deeds surrounding Direction – *Where* you want to go and *how* to get there.

Specific actions

Once you know your brief, list the key decision makers and ask yourself what do they need to know from you?

- Is it your philosophy/style of play?
- Your opinion of where the club is now, and where you think the team can go?
- Are changes to the squad required?
- What is the current level of perceived ability of the squad?
- What does the culture you are trying to build look like?

You must communicate clearly what your intentions are for the next three, six, and nine months; and how you intend to build the club moving forward. At a professional level, this includes the Chairman, Boardroom, Immediate Department Staff, etc. At a recreational level, this may mean a brief meeting with parents, players, and sponsors. *Whatever* the level, an increase in clear communication creates a sense of certainty; certainty creates confidence, and confidence drives performance.

Exercises

Jot down the agreed goals and subsequent action plan required to achieve your objectives.

For example, one agreed goal could be promotion. So, the action plan could look like:

- How did the team do last year?
- What did they do well?
- Where do they need to be significantly better?
- What does the league or level demand?
- What is the current competition?
- What got in the way of promotion last year?
- What players do we need to sign next? Goalkeeper, Central Midfielder, Striker, etc.
- Is it realistic to be working for promotion this year? If it's not promotion, think about the following...

  o What are our objectives this year?
  o What are the current variables and resources that may help or hinder the achievement of this goal?
  o What would I need to change, improve, or add, to make this goal achievable?
  o What needs to change immediately as a non-negotiable?
  o What needs to stay the same?

Having pinpointed these issues, determine the first five things you need to do to get the ball rolling? E.g.

- Meet with the Director of Football to establish style of play
- Agree your budget with the owner with identified targets
- Assemble your immediate coaching team and supporting multi-disciplinary specialists
- Identify and agree the season's expectations
- Lead a staff meeting to communicate your plan of action

Recruitment, Evaluation and Analysis

Draw up a list of current players and a recent history of the team's success. What are the strengths and weaknesses associated with the current team and squad of players? Where do you need to add? Who are the 'development players' within the team who you can work with to improve? Who simply has to go?

If possible, make a statistical assessment of each player including goals, assists, clean sheets, distances run, etc. With data, you can evaluate players more objectively; data can underpin your development plan offered to the board, the Director of Football, or senior executive team.

Data analysis can assist you in making factual decisions based on statistical evaluation. This is important for two reasons; firstly sometimes data patterns and trends can help us build a clearer picture of a player's effectiveness. Secondly, coaching is both an art *and a science*. A coach's intuition is important in evaluating strengths and weaknesses but, in combination with objective measurement and analysis, a more accurate account of performance can be built.

Relationships

Who are the people who are going to support you in making the club's ambition a reality? Who are the dream stealers and mood hoovers, in comparison to the solution-orientated activists and energy givers?

Every individual within your team is unique with different personalities, and preferences. Creating, building and maintaining successful relationships will require you to understand each player, and each staff member – getting to know them as people.

In order to create the most effective team, understanding the strengths and weaknesses of your staff is as crucial as understanding the strengths and weaknesses of the players. Some will be extremely organised and detailed, others irresistibly charismatic and inspiring. As the head coach, trusting your staff to deliver their work creates a trust between you and them. As the head coach, you also have to manage your energy and be fresh when you need to be, to maximise your effectiveness.

Creating clear roles and responsibilities for who is doing 'what, when, and why' can help to create a collective shared mental model. Systemically, when each individual feels connected, certain and valued, with a clear opportunity to contribute, successful 'ways of working' can be created. From sports science to analysis, the coaching team to recruitment, establishing effective and authentic relationships is a fundamental ingredient in building the chemistry and autonomy required to succeed together.

Mission and Purpose

The thing I want to achieve and *why* I want to achieve it.

Story

What's your message? One of the most powerful things a coach needs to consider is what key message he or she wishes to communicate. For example, a coach taking over a team built around a strong squad with effective playing personnel might believe that it's important to reinforce the belief that promotion is the number one target.

A coach taking over a team in a relegation position with ten games to go may want to highlight the key strategy of staying up or inspiring the team to focus on winning beliefs.

Setting the scene with the story, and communicating it clearly and regularly, acts to bind everyone together in a common sense of purpose.

One Director of Coaching recently held a club-wide meeting with a professional team I was working with. He presented for one hour to every staff member in the club with one theme; *we all help the team win on Saturday*. The staff left the coaches' meeting feeling energised and connected to one main theme. Regardless of our roles, however big or small they may seem, in some way, we all help the team to win on Saturday.

Character Counts

Tony Dungy, a former head coach of the NFL Indianapolis Colts, ran player trials with a checklist for his coaches to assess players' suitability to join the team.

Amongst the list of technical, tactical, and physical capabilities, there was a tick box at the end of the assessment paper labelled 'DNDC' which stood for 'Do Not Draft Due to Character'. Quite simply, Tony believed that character was a defining aspect of a player's make up.

Using the simple and easy matrix below, you can assess the characters in your team.

Assessing Character

Leaders	Chameleons
The professional warriors who set standards and drive performance on and off the pitch. These characters do the right thing every day no matter what. They do what is right, not what is easy.	The ones who change with the wind and adapt based on where the power base lies. These characters can be positively or negatively persuaded based on the strength of the influence.
Terrorists	**Lone Rangers**
These negative influences purposefully undermine and damage the health of the team through their destructive attitude and poisonous behaviour.	Characters who detach themselves from the crowd and remain independent of any one group. They inherently prefer to keep a distance and remain separated.

Once you've categorised your personnel, take a step back and evaluate the balance. How many Leaders do you have compared to Terrorists? How can you re-engage the Lone Rangers and ensure the Chameleons remain positively influenced?

Understanding Self, Understanding the Situation

Finally, using the simple SWOT analysis tool below, you will be able to evaluate your club, your team, and your situation more effectively.

What are the Strengths, Weaknesses, Opportunities, and Threats associated with taking on the job? This can be done on two levels. One for yourself as a self-analysis task, and the other for the team or club you have just taken over.

SWOT Analysis – Self Analysis

Strengths	Weaknesses
Opportunities	Threats

SWOT Analysis – The Club

Strengths	Weaknesses
Opportunities	Threats

Summary

Understanding the job you were recruited for means having absolute clarity regarding yourself, your role, and your responsibility. The enemy of clarity is confusion. Confusion will ultimately and inevitably lead to failure.

As the coach, one of your top-most priorities is to get clear about where you are, what you're doing, and why. As a coach, you must fuel your players' feelings of certainty, and engage the interest of your team, giving them the best possible chance of achieving their goals.

When you kill confusion through clarity, you create a framework for accountability to flourish.

Getting *clear* about the job you were brought in to do is more than strategy, roles, and responsibilities. Getting *clear* will give you a sense of conviction and positive feeling of direction. When you're *clear* about *where* you are, *what* you're doing, *where* you're going, and *why* – you're giving yourself and your team the best possible chance to succeed.

PRINCIPLE 3
BUILDING A POSITIVE ATTITUDE

Performance is defined by attitude, and attitude is a choice. Champions choose their attitudes wisely. A positive, healthy, winning attitude – enabling an individual to stay focused, confident, and ready – is the hallmark of a true champion.

> **You are what your deep driving desire is.**
>
> **As your desire is, so is your will.**
>
> **As your will is, so is your deed.**
>
> **As your deed is, so is your destiny**
>
> Brihadaranyaka Upanishad IV.4.5

Champions live out a winning attitude in their lives by:

- Taking responsibility for their success and failures.
- Accepting that there are always areas for improvement.
- Welcoming constructive criticism.
- Ruthlessly working hard to improve.
- Taking ownership of their personal progress plans.
- Constantly reflecting on self and performance.

Michael Jordan

If we want to look at attitude, let's take the story of the most iconic basketball hero the world has ever seen. Many people attribute his success to some God-given talent – something innate that produced such a naturally gifted and superior athlete.

Surely people don't develop *those* sorts of abilities, do they?

What most of us don't know, however, was that Michael was not always thought of as the best. Cut from the starting squad of the 1978 Emsley A. Laney High School varsity basketball team, Michael was told he needed more experience and wasn't tall enough. Having failed to secure one of the 15 places available, he was sent to play his sophomore year at junior varsity before he could make the high school squad.

It was this very moment that Michael looks back on, remembering the significance of that failure as the birth of his inner resolve for his life ahead. "It was embarrassing not making the team. My mum told me that the only thing to do is prove to the coach that he had made a mistake and that's what I did."

In fact, every morning at 6.00 am, Michael would arrive at the basketball court early for practice ahead of the coach and the team. "Whenever I was working out or got tired and figured I ought to stop, I'd close my eyes and see that list in the locker room without my name on it. That usually got me going again."

Using that momentary setback as the very motivation to succeed, Jordan went on to score multiple 40-point games and attracted unprecedented crowds in his very first junior varsity sophomore year.

Michael Jordan offers us these lessons:

- A moment of failure is another great reason to succeed.
- You can achieve incomparable levels of skill through incomparable levels of spirit and commitment.
- A dream can become a reality with unrelenting perseverance and purposeful practice.
- The journey of performance excellence is a path of constant and never-ending improvement.

> **Michael is a genius who constantly wants to upgrade on his genius.**
>
> John Bach

Attitude Drives Performance

It was about 6:45 am on a cold and wet rainy morning when I arrived at Birmingham City FC's training ground ahead of what was going to be a long day of work.

I was extra early that day because it was a Tuesday, and Tuesday meant evening youth team training. The only way I could fit a personal gym session into the day (I try to look after myself!) was if I arrived before the first-team boys and all the other staff.

I did the maths in my head and figured I'd have about an hour and 15 minutes before the gym became active and my day's work would begin with the U18s in their morning technical session. I used to like training on my own in the gym early in the morning. There was a stillness about the weights and the mats, as if they were waking up themselves… welcoming me in.

Today was different though.

Today, unknown to me, was going to be the day that I learnt a very powerful lesson, delivered by a 16-year-old boy fixed with a dream, breaking the early morning silence not through speech but with action. There, lying down on the mats, with sweat dripping off his forehead lay a player who would – unbeknown to all of us – impact the future of the first team in ways we did not comprehend.

There, lying down on the mats, lay the shape of a player who was different. Not in physical stature but in mental strength. It was 6:45 am and here was a player who was showing his class and character not in loud words but with great action. On the gym wall, behind him, was a poignant affirmation, one of many but particularly relevant.

"The vision of a champion is someone who is bent over exhausted, dripping with sweat, when no-one is watching." Anson Dorrance

That was Nathan. This was the moment I realised that this 16-year-old talent was extra-ordinary, a cut above the rest, different. He was what Malcolm Gladwell would term *an outlier*.

The much-loved John Wooden quote "Ability may get you to the top, but it takes character to keep you there" was the first concept we discussed in our very first session together. I could tell from the depth of Nathan's concentrated gaze that he was fast-forwarding into the future. Muhammad Ali once said, "The fight is won or lost far away from witnesses… long before I dance under those lights" and I could tell from the way Nathan tuned his focus into every single session that he was prepared to be different. He was prepared to think outside the box; prepared to do what others would not in order to achieve what others could not; prepared to open up his mind, his heart, his deeper dreams and ambitions and in the process be unafraid of sharing them.

Nathan Redmond reminded me of the famous story about NFL quarterback Tom Brady. In the 2000 NFL draft, Tom Brady (who would become the greatest the sport had ever encountered) was overlooked and picked only in the sixth round by the Patriots at number 199/200. Six quarterbacks were picked in front of him. Several scouting reports detailed his physical, technical, and tactical deficiencies, and reported clear limits on his potential, and lack of ability to play at the highest level.

So the obvious question arises. How is it that such a magnificent talent could be so easily missed? Head Coach of the San Francisco 49ers from

1997-2002, Steve Mariucci, explains the fundamental flaw in the NFL recruitment process. "We didn't open up his chest and look at his heart; I don't know if anybody did."

Once again, the major and essential ingredients required for high achievement emerge not in apparent talent or skill, but the recesses of the mind and in the depths of the heart.

The longer I live, the more I realise the impact of attitude on life. Attitude is to me, more important than facts.

It is more important than the past, than education, than money, than circumstances, than failure, than successes, than what other people think or say or do. It is more important than appearances, giftedness, or skill. It will make or break a company, a church, a home.

The remarkable thing is we have a choice every day regarding the attitude we will embrace for the day.

We cannot change our past – we cannot change the fact that people will act in a certain way. We cannot change the inevitable. The only thing we can do is play on the one string we have, and that is attitude.

I am convinced that life is 10% of what happens to us, and 90% how we react to it. And so it is with you – we are in charge of our attitudes.

Charles Swindoll

Beckham's Brilliance

David Beckham is another sportsman with something special inside. Arguably one of England's finest footballers, at international level, he holds the most caps for any outfield player (115), he captained England for six years, and scored in three World Cups. With Manchester United, he won the Premier League six times, gained two FA Cups, and the UEFA Champions League. His success abroad saw him win the La Liga title with the 'Galacticos' at Real Madrid, whilst in the US he won the Major League Soccer Cup twice with LA Galaxy before finishing his career with loan spells at AC Milan and Paris Saint-Germain.

That level of sustained success is certainly not by accident.

Beckham's brilliance is, by his own admission, an attitude. "If you want to improve, you have to keep pushing yourself," he declared. This was particularly evident during the 2010-11 season when – during a winter break from the MLS – Beckham chose to train with Tottenham Hotspur FC. I'll never forget standing with my friend Anthony Hudson (the then U23s assistant coach) watching whilst David Beckham trained.

It was a masterclass in Attitude and Drive.

He touched the ball twice as often as anyone else, made more telling and precise passes that penetrated the opposition, and covered more distance with energy than any other player on show. To cap it off, when the rest of the team went in, guess who stayed out to practice some more? 25 free kicks with his left foot and 25 free kicks with his right. This training attitude to 'do more, be more' offers significant evidence that even after all his success, Beckham's brilliance on the field was down to his outstanding drive, fuelled by an attitude for constant improvement.

*

Some players, like Nathan, Tom Brady, and David Beckham, have an inner determination that is not seen in every player – even if every player aspires to emulate these champions. One of the reasons attitude is not more pervasive is the prevalence of its evil twin: self-doubt.

> **Doubt kills more dreams than failure ever will.**
>
> Suzy Kassem

England Ladies U23 and Birmingham City FC centre-forward Kirsty Linnett was an athlete stricken with self-doubt until she found a renewed sense of empowerment. I first came across Kirsty when she was 20-years-old. She explained that she was at a really low point after being out for almost two years with back-to-back ACL reconstructions. She was breaking down physically on the pitch, and her self-esteem was at its lowest. Indeed, the negative thoughts she once had caused her to walk off the pitch in the middle of a match. She was not enjoying the game she loved playing from a young age.

Kirsty was convinced she'd get injured again. She had fallen foul to a self-imposed, negative downward spiral of self-doubt. She knew she had to break the pattern. Together we developed a series of coping strategies which she worked hard to hone and embed into her game. When bad thoughts started in her mind, instead of self-doubt undermining her performance as it once had, she would start to take over and stop it. This is how Kirsty did it.

Kirsty's Mind Gym Exercises – 6 keys that led to positive change

1. Is that really true?

Kirsty and I actively questioned and challenged thoughts of self-doubt by asking "Where is the evidence this thought is true?" For example, to the thought "I'm going to get injured again I just know it," we would ask "how do we know?" It may sound simple, but by questioning negative thoughts openly with a thinking partner, one is able to consciously interrupt a negative pattern of self-doubt and open a space for new, more empowering beliefs to replace the old dysfunctional ones. "I've trained hard to strengthen my knee in rehab, I'm stronger than ever right now," is a more authentic and empowering thought. It boosts self-belief.

2. Commitment to Action

In creating an action plan that led to specific and measurable strengthening exercises for her knee, Kirsty eliminated self-doubt through *physical action*. With every rep, she focused more on the strength and power in her knee. As she moved closer to peak physical condition, she shifted her focus from rehabilitative recovery to asking a much more empowering question: "How strong can I possibly become?"

3. Visualise to Materialise

Through the use of imagery, Kirsty created an ideal vision of herself. By imagining how her most confident self would look, think, feel and perform, she painted a powerful self-portrait. With each visualisation, she reinforced the positive emotions associated with her image.

4. Gratitude Changes Attitude

By focusing her cognitive energy on the things that she felt sincerely grateful for, in her life, Kirsty developed a new emotional energy. In counting her blessings in the present, she released the burdens of the past.

5. Getting a Thinking Partner

Working out in the mind gym can get lonely. Through speaking out, sharing, and discussing perceived problems, Kirsty acted to release the tension that might build up when things get held in. This 'cognitive catharsis' is a type of valve that acts to release the mental pressure that can build up when we shut ourselves off.

6. The Energy Team

In one of the sessions that Kirsty and I spent together, we drew a line down the middle of a white A4 piece of paper with a plus sign on one side and a minus sign on the other. The whole focus of the session was to think of all of the people, places, and things that existed in her life that gave her energy and all of the things that took her energy away. At the end of the session, she left with the challenge of making real and positive changes by removing the energy vampires from her life, and increasing the influence of her energy team. In this way, we were able to work on personal and performance development together and top up the energy tank.

Through working hard in the mind gym, Kirsty managed to restore her self-esteem and find renewed levels of confidence and belief once again. Sure enough, performances followed, and she found herself back involved at International level with the England U23's. Kirsty is now playing in the senior Women's Premier League for Reading FC.

Specific actions

Make a list of the top five traits you want your players to live out through their attitudes.

(Example) I want my players to:

1. Lead by example, with passion and positivity despite setbacks.
2. Maintain hope and signpost success with encouragement.
3. Breed belief by fuelling each other with faith and optimism.
4. Remain determined together.
5. Constantly want to improve, learn, and develop.

My top five traits – *I want my players to*:

1.	
2.	
3.	
4.	
5.	

Once you've developed your list, now ask yourself the question: "What can I do to instil these traits in my players?" Make your list below.

Example:

1. Make sure I pick positive aspects of performance out of a negative result and highlight these to the players, using a ratio of 3:1 (positive to negative).
2. Live with energy and encourage my players when praise is deserved.
3. Show and tell my players why I believe in them, using specific examples.
4. Banish doubt and protect my players from negative people.
5. Keep learning myself; commit to a course to improve my own skill set.

Now make your list below.

What can I do to instil these traits in my players?

1.	
2.	
3.	
4.	
5.	

From Negative to Positive

Clearly, not all players possess a naturally positive attitude. Coaches need to recognise that attitude can be taught. Like any other skill, it can be learned. Attitude is a mental muscle – the more you work it, the stronger it becomes.

I remember coming back from a Premier League U18s fixture one Saturday and sitting next to a player who had just received a fair amount of direct criticism from his coach after a 0-5 loss to Arsenal away in the league. This particular player didn't cope well when things went against him. He reacted badly to constructive criticism and played the victim by blaming others for his own poor performance. This is a classic defensive habit for self-protection to avoid the pain and discomfort of owning the responsibility to improve. Basic victim mentality – "It wasn't *my* fault."

This particular coach journey was going to be different. As one of the assistant coaches, I asked the analyst to share his laptop and pick out the exact moments that led to the mistakes the player made in the game.

I asked the player three simple questions.

1. What do you see?
2. What were you thinking?
3. How did you feel?

Here were the player's responses:

1. I didn't see the player (*who won the ball that led to the conceded goal*) behind me…
2. I thought I had more time and space than I actually did…
3. I felt shocked, panicked, and couldn't recover…

What the player was actually telling me was:

1. He didn't see the player behind him (*spatial awareness and scanning ability*).
2. He thought he had more time and space (*speed and efficiency of his decision-making skills*).
3. He was panicked (*emotional control and composure*).

When I presented these three skills back to the player and offered some simple sessions to improve the three skills – his attitude shifted. Here's why.

As coaches, we must understand the need for both *challenge* and *support*.

PRINCIPLE 3

The Challenge and Support Matrix

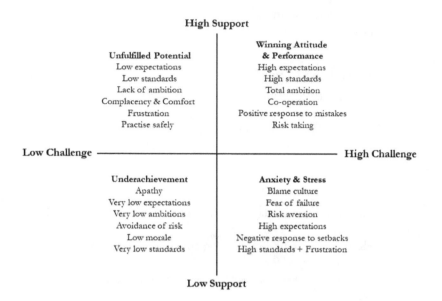

High Support

Unfulfilled Potential	Winning Attitude & Performance
Low expectations	High expectations
Low standards	High standards
Lack of ambition	Total ambition
Complacency & Comfort	Co-operation
Frustration	Positive response to mistakes
Practise safely	Risk taking

Low Challenge ———————————————— **High Challenge**

Underachievement	Anxiety & Stress
Apathy	Blame culture
Very low expectations	Fear of failure
Very low ambitions	Risk aversion
Avoidance of risk	High expectations
Low morale	Negative response to setbacks
Very low standards	High standards + Frustration

Low Support

The combination and connection between the two is as critical to comprehend as the formation that you play. If you provide an environment rich in support and which is highly challenging, you breed a confident, risk-taking player who takes responsibility, with a winning attitude that drives performance. If you offer all the support in the world but the players are simply not challenged, they will never fulfil their true potential. If the challenge is high, but players feel there is no support, they will be anxious and ultimately fear the defining moments in training and matches. Only when the player knows that the coach will provide a constant challenge – whilst offering support and guidance in equal measure – can they express their true potential.

As coaches, we have to be investigators, digging beneath the surface of the obvious first behaviour.

Let's take the example of the above player whose attitude was considered poor by the head coach. He showed no signs of improving and *always* blamed others around him for his own mistakes. But, in actual fact, turning this player's 'poor attitude' into a positive one, was about understanding where he was in the matrix. Did the coach challenge the player? Yes. Did he offer support, guidance, and training to meet the challenges? No! The result was 'poor attitude'.

When we, as coaches, take a step back using the (above) grid to gain perspective and understand context, we can see how to turn this player's attitude from negative to positive. In training later that week, the head coach arranged an individual meeting with the player, designed a programme to improve the three key skills (Spatial Awareness and Scanning, Speed Efficiency of Decision Making, Emotional Control and Composure), and reinforced his support to help the player meet the challenge.

Summary

The attitude of your team has the power to create or destroy a practice, a match, or a season. Building a healthy, positive, winning attitude for your team starts with your capacity as the coach to set the standards yourself. In living out the beliefs and behaviours you hold most dear, you signpost your environment by modelling your attitude. In other words, attitude reflects leadership. As the coach and leader, your job is to build positive attitude in your players, so they fulfil their true potential.

PRINCIPLE 4
A LEADER'S LANDSCAPE

> **People don't buy what you do; they buy why you do it.**
> Simon Sinek

A culture of excellence is built upon a firm foundation of core values, and all who buy into it are required to live and breathe them. A culture of excellence is a place that demands the very best from you; at the same time, you know only your best will be good enough for it.

In his magnificent book, *Legacy*, James Kerr encourages readers to delve into the cultural depths of the New Zealand All Blacks Rugby Team, revealing the key values that shape the very fabric of their environment. During the six weeks he spent living and studying the team, he learnt about the power of humility and the transformational influence this core value creates.

"Humility begins at the level of interpersonal communication, enabling an interrogative, highly facilitated learning environment in which no-one has all the answers. Each individual is invited to contribute solutions to the challenges being posed. This is a key component of building sustainable competitive advantage through cultural cohesion."

It's important to note that this book is about the practical application and experiential nature of high performance as opposed to academic theory. It is also an attempt to capture some of the real-life challenges and triumphs that sportsmen and sportswomen have encountered along the way. So, let's start by examining the value of clarity.

Clarity - The Catalyst for Confidence

When learning about the experiences of sporting successes, the importance of clarity and its relationship with confidence has shone through. For a coach, it is the ability to be clear about what needs to be done – to get the result – that matters. In turn, coaches who are able to be clear and calm, breed confidence in their players.

The linear relationship between these two components is simple but profound. The clearer you can be about what is required (exactly) of your players, the more confidently they will be able to perform. That means clarity in relation to roles and responsibilities within the team and training plans, but also emotional, psychological clarity. When players feel they have clarity about who you are, and what you stand for, they will be stable and secure within themselves. They will be certain and ready to perform when it matters.

Clarity = Confidence

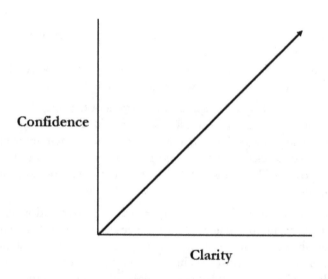

Coaches who are clear with their communication style create players who are confident, certain, and clear.

- Confident about their roles and responsibilities within the team.
- Certain about the core values, beliefs, and expectations of the coach.
- Clear, emotionally, about their connection to the team and how they can contribute to it.
- Clear, psychologically, about strategy, tactics and the game plan.

A coach who is clear in the way they communicate creates confidence in their players. Players who are confident about themselves and their potential, are players who win in their minds.

Here are three simple tools you can adopt to ensure clarity breeds confidence in your players:

The Power of Three

Chunk your information down into three key points in team meetings or half-time team talks. By making three central points, you prioritise the key messages, making it easier for the players to absorb and process the most important information. It's not about how much you know as the coach; it's about how much the players are ready and able to take on board.

There's a very important psychological truth behind the power of three, and it's widely recognised in marketing and politics. It is no accident that the use of 'three' finds itself playing a central role in some of our greatest stories, children's fairy tales, and myths: the three little pigs, the three musketeers, and the three blind mice. On the Olympic stage, we celebrate gold, silver, and bronze, and Hollywood screenwriters normally have a three-act structure.

Three just so happens to be the smallest number needed to create a pattern, and the human brain has had to evolve to become efficient at pattern recognition. There's a reason why "Life, liberty, and the pursuit of happiness" was Thomas Jefferson's choice of words when the USA's Declaration of Independence was drafted. Some of the most successful corporate marketing campaigns have been delivered using the power of three. Think of famous food slogans like the one for breakfast cereal Rice Krispies and its "Snap, Crackle, and Pop", or possibly one of the most famous marketing slogans of all time… Nike's three words: "Just Do It".

When you present information to your players using the power of three, you give them the opportunity to digest, remember, and act on your instruction.

Use of Questions

When you employ open questions with your players, you reinforce learning and cement key objectives. Giving your players the opportunity to summarise and clarify information enables you to evaluate the level of individual and collective understanding.

Offering a closed question like "Do you understand?" only gives the player a two option response: "yes" or "no".

Using an open question such as "What do you understand?" enables them to express and share their own level of comprehension. As the coach, it gives you the chance to assess understanding but also open a new avenue for developing social confidence through player communication.

Pictures paint a thousand words

Players learn in different ways. Using a tactics board, poster print, or flip chart to break down simple key points will assist your players in staying focused and maintaining concentration. Pictures and videos which emphasise central learning points will also act to illustrate and underpin the information you want to convey.

The Separation of Performance from Identity

> **He made me feel safe, confident, good enough to play for Man Utd. He made me feel as if I was the most important one.**
>
> Phil Neville on Sir Alex Ferguson

Cultural leaders have magical ways of making people feel valued and significant; it enables individuals to be connected and contribute to the team, to the organisation. One of the ways, I've learned that this happens is when people learn they are more than the outcome. In sport, it would be easy to base someone's *worth* on whether they win or lose, play well or play badly. Win and play well and you're valuable. Lose or play badly and your worth diminishes. This is, in fact, one of the harsh realities of the football industry.

But what if this reality has been formed with short-sightedness? What if there was another way in which we could measure and therefore develop talent and potential? What if we could create a culture that fosters a longer-term approach not based on short-term outcomes, but on long-term potential? What if we could design a living, breathing culture that is built on a philosophy of sustainable personal enrichment (and not a short-term snapshot judgement)?

One of the ways I've seen this done skilfully was whilst working at West Bromwich Albion. Academy Manager Mark Harrison led a post-match de-brief with the U18's following a 3-1 away defeat to Peterborough United, a match that a Premier League Academy is always expected to win. After summarising three key areas of the game tactically, Mark finished his team talk with a simple phrase clearly and calmly: "We weren't good enough today." In essence, to the observer, this phrase might appear similar to any other dressing room coach-led debrief. But study the hidden detail of this phrase and we will quickly see a far greater – more intelligent – deliberate dynamic at play.

Firstly, like all good coaches, Mark didn't say *you* were not good enough today, he said *we*. What did the players learn? That the coach is part of the team's success and he also owns failure. Big lesson.

Secondly, and perhaps more crucially, he said, "We weren't good enough *today*." Compare that for a second with, "You are not good enough." Do you feel the immediate difference? One is a defining statement of ability and identity based on the short-term outcome of losing. The other is an inclusive short-term statement that separates performance from identity and suggests positive improvement is possible. Although simple and sometimes difficult to detect, these words contain the ingredients to go beyond the short-termism of outcome-based talent judgement, and points toward a greater vision of true growth and potential. Message? Failure is not final. We can improve together, over time.

Gareth Southgate – A New England Culture for the Three Lions

It's a wet, grey spring day and the rain has just begun to fall. But as I walk into the National Football Centre, I can't help but feel inspired by the surroundings. The rain glistens off the immaculately cut grass pitches and just through the entrance to headquarters, there are England shirts hanging on the wall that date back over the years. Today, however, I'm interested not by the past but the present; specifically, the high-performance culture emerging from the FA's renewed sense of football evolution, due in no small part to its Director of Elite Talent Development, Dan Ashworth.

Sitting with Dan, the topic of our conversation is dominated by a common curiosity around the evolving landscape of high-performance culture in professional football. "Society has changed and will change again," Dan explained. "Change is constant. We need to understand the forces that shape that societal change and adapt to best respond to the needs of our players and our staff." The new era of modern-day leadership and management requires different skills today than for 20 years ago. That much is true.

This need to understand societal pressures is a theme that is carried forward by England coach, Gareth Southgate. He tells me he feels the dynamics of education and family life is different now compared to 10 years ago. Authority is questioned a lot more. In sport and education, coaches need to be able to explain *what* they're doing and *why*. People don't just follow leaders now because they are the 'leader'. They don't blindly follow anyone anywhere. The leaders of the today are the ones who create a vision that their followers feel *compelled* to follow. Leaders must tap into the individual motivations of their players because player ownership and accountability are the driving forces of today's high-performance cultures.

In truth, in an era when absolute dictatorial leadership is dying, in all walks of life, without a doubt the successful high-performance culture of tomorrow will be defined by the leaders who think more about the virtues of human development than any other aspect. If a culture is indeed defined by the people, then an investment in, and understanding of, those people must be at the heart of its growth.

Specific actions

As we affirmed in Principle 1, seeing the world through the eyes of your players creates empathy, understanding, and trust. As coach, you are also responsible for ensuring there is a healthy respect within the team by setting clear standards for behaviour and performance. These actions may feel similar in nature but it is important to reinforce these principles systematically to create a consistent culture.

Five key steps for building a healthy relationship with your team:

1. Clarify the non-negotiables in your agreed standards and code of conduct; these should include: timekeeping, expectations, and behaviours.
2. Set up a meeting where every player and coach has the opportunity to contribute and share their ideas. It is essential that each person feels that they are an important contributing member.
3. Build authentic trust by being genuinely interested in the person behind the player or staff member. Find out three key facts about their lives, where they were born, their interests, and needs.
4. Create shared ownership opportunities by asking questions such as "How do you feel we should respond in games when this happens?" Write these ideas up and make them visible in the dressing room. This creates shared ownership and accountability. "Here's what we agreed on…"
5. Share the success and the temporary failures of the team. Never separate yourself from your players in times of difficulty.

> With intelligent hard work, each can achieve the best that is within him or within his team, and this is the standard he will be measured by, both by other persons and by himself.
>
> James 'Doc' Counsilman

Set standards

> You can't get to courage without walking through vulnerability.
>
> Brené Brown

In Patrick Lencioni's famous leadership fable *The 5 Dysfunctions of a Team*, he explores the fundamental causes of internal politics and organisational failure. The first dysfunction is illustrated as a *lack of trust* born out of an inability to be vulnerable amongst peers, ultimately arising in a fear of conflict.

The following exercise is designed as a simple non-threatening platform for honest self-reflection and team disclosure.

As the coach, bring the team together as a whole or invite them in their units broken up into: Goalkeepers, Defenders, Midfielders, and Attackers.

1. Each player offers three things to the group: name, major strengths, a professional area for improvement.
2. Give the players three minutes each to present to whomever is present. This is a trust-building, rapport-enacting exercise. No excuses, no hiding places. No-one's perfect, everyone has something they can improve.
3. Create an opportunity for each player to write down or speak out a plan of action "This is how I would improve .... 1, 2, 3..."
4. Provide an example of a tactical, technical, mental/emotional, personal/lifestyle action plan for players to relate to.
5. Schedule a regular opportunity for players to share progress and development plans to sustain and foster a learning environment.

Summary

As we have discovered through endless research and valuable experience, effective leadership in the future will require a new set of skills to adapt to the ever-changing coaching landscape.

It will require coaches to realise the need to separate performance from identity, measuring 'success' on development rather than outcome.

Becoming an effective guide in the facilitation of learning will enable the future coach to discover hidden depths of player potential. A greater emphasis on the creation of player-led co-created environments will not mean the absence of (or lack of need for) traditional coach-led direction. It will, however, require recognition of the 'shifts' in importance, priority, and context for a coach's actions, to maximise their effectiveness. In other words, the future coach will still need to wear different hats at different times, but certain hats will be required to be worn for longer.

Becoming a coach that can communicate with clarity in the direction and purpose of their mission will appeal to the new age of intelligence. But, in this new age, a strong sense of moral integrity will remain at the heart of coaching, at all ages and levels the game.

PRINCIPLE 5
CONFIDENCE AND CULTURE

> **A nation's culture resides in the heart and soul of its people.**
> Mahatma Gandhi

A culture of excellence is built upon a firm foundation of core values that everyone who buys into it is required to live and breathe. A culture of excellence is a place that demands the very best from you. At the same time, you know only your best will be good enough for it. Each club and each team will possess unique personnel with different characteristics and experiences; building your culture requires you to glue, blend, and sculpt those differences into one collective shared vision.

In Principle 5, you must identify the existing culture, determine the new culture you want, and implement it.

What is a 'Fear of Failure'?

> **It is impossible to live without failing at something, unless you live so cautiously that you might as well not have lived at all – in which case, you fail by default.**
> J.K. Rowling

A fear of failure is a force that can keep a winning mind closed. A fear of failure can be a reason why some players stop pursuing their dreams and stop taking calculated risks.

- What if it doesn't work out?
- What if I look stupid?
- What if I have to fail over and over again before I get there?
- What if people think of me as a failure?
- What if I give it my very best shot and still end up falling short of the mark?

- What does that mean about me?

Fear likes to attach itself to a particular way of thinking, which creates a fixed frame of mind. It's a pessimistic voice that likes to predict undesirable outcomes, which leads to a no risk mentality. Because of fear, people want to avoid the perceived pain associated with falling short.

People with a fear of failure focus on the threat in the situation and neglect to acknowledge methods of coping or control. Those threats might relate to reputation, 'what will they think about me'; a physical threat, 'I might get hurt'; or an emotional threat, 'I'm not strong enough to cope'. Although most players and coaches with this fixed mindset desperately desire different results, they aren't courageous enough to change their thinking to create these results. And we know that two of the key drivers of positive and lasting change are the capacity to think differently and act differently.

In order to reach new levels of performance, to achieve new heights, coaches must be prepared to consider alternative perspectives in order to evolve and advance. Critically perhaps, there are three inevitabilities in relation to the process of a coach's evolution:

1. It is impossible to progress without being brave enough to try new things.
2. Not all new ideas will be 'better' ideas. The *process* is highly valuable.
3. When implementing new ideas, there may be an initial stage of 'failure'.

He who is not courageous enough to take risks will accomplish nothing in life.

Muhammad Ali

If we see failure as a negative, destructive, and definable aspect of ourselves – our performances, careers, and lives will always be limited. Instead of living out our dreams, we will live within the restrictions of our accepted fears. Our job should be to replace these fears with constant acts of courage in action.

Choice in Challenge

Imagine you have a choice. Two sweets: one blue and one red.

If you choose the blue sweet, you'll never fail again for the rest of your life. If you choose the red sweetie, you'll continue to face setbacks, challenges, make mistakes, and encounter the struggles that everyday life presents.

You're tempted by the blue sweet aren't you? I mean who wants to continue to face constant setbacks and failures? Who wishes to be branded a loser?

The blue/red sweet deal was presented to a group of eight-year-old girls, at a prestigious London school. Nearly all of them chose the blue sweet. The Headmistress, Heather Hanbury, offered an explanation behind her students' choices: "They have been afraid of getting things wrong." When you think about that for a short while, it makes logical sense doesn't it? No-one actually wants to suffer, do they? Everyone wants to succeed.

Unfortunately, there are no blue sweets. Life and football have a habit of only dishing out the red ones. It is important that we help players not to be afraid to face challenges and setbacks in their pursuit of excellence. In other words, to coach players not to be afraid of failure but to welcome it.

On a UEFA coaching course, in 2013, fellow candidate and ex-Manchester United coach and player Phil Neville explained why he believed a cluster of great young players emerged from Manchester United's youth team in 1992. "When I look back at Ryan Giggs, Gary (Neville), Paul Scholes, David Beckham, Nicky Butt, and myself, we shared common traits. We constantly challenged each other in training and in the gym. We never left a single stone unturned in our preparation and loved a difficult challenge. I think when you're surrounded by characters like that, every day becomes another chance to improve."

Notice that Phil was seeking out the challenges. He didn't avoid them. He went after them, and the further outside his comfort zone he travelled, the greater progress he stood to make. He was actively overcoming any fear of failure he felt by facing up to it, seeking it out, and responding with courage in action. As the brilliant book written by Susan Jeffers would suggest, he was *feeling* the fear and *doing* it anyway. (The book was called *Feel The Fear And Do It Anyway!*)

PRINCIPLE 5

> ## I am always doing that which I cannot do in order that I may learn how to do it.
> Pablo Picasso

When you think about it, failure isn't that scary in its most simple form. We fail every day at all sorts of things: burning the toast, arriving late to a meeting, forgetting to pick milk up on the way home – the list is endless.

Whilst burning the toast is somewhat trivial, let's up the stakes a little. Let's say you've got to give a presentation to the five most important people at work and your job depends on whether you make a 'success' of it or not. In other words, if they're not impressed with your work then you're sacked. Suddenly, real consequences are at play (unemployment, lack of income, no money for the mortgage), and herein lies the underlying issue. It's not the actual event (underperforming in a presentation) it's the associated set of *perceived* negative consequences that causes anxiety to arise. It is the fear of what failure will mean, rather than failure itself that inhibits performance.

It is the same for players. It is the perception of what failure means that holds them back. To see this more clearly, consider how players answer the following questions:

- What if I'm dropped from the team?
- What if I make a mistake in training?
- What if I don't make the starting 11?

A player's response will tell us a great deal about what failure means to them.

A player who fears failure is likely to respond with:

- I am not a good footballer.
- I can't play well enough.
- I will never make it.

On the other hand, a player who welcomes failure will react differently to these 'what if's:

- This setback is temporary. I can improve!
- I will learn from this; I will work harder!

- I'm a fighter; I can respond to any situation!

We can think of this player as having a Response-*ABLE* mindset. They respond in a way that enables them to move forward, make improvements, and continue to strive towards excellence no matter what setbacks they face.

The key question is how can we help players move from having a fear of failure to welcoming it? First, we need to understand what makes up a Response-*ABLE* mindset.

Ingredients of a Response-*ABLE* Mindset

Grit

There are certain patterns that I witness time and time again with elite players. A certain set of defining qualities that endure under any circumstance and which can be grouped under the term 'inner steel'. It's a classifying trait of a true champion. The pure refusal to quit, give up, or give in. The ultimate voice of inner perseverance that reaffirms the desire to keep moving forward no matter how tough it gets. This voice isn't always a loud deafening roar; sometimes it's a whisper that says gently 'try again tomorrow'. It's courage that displays itself in one's actions rather than their words.

Professor Angela Duckworth, from the University of Pennsylvania, called this inner quality *grit*. She examined the ingredients for success in students, and the key to success turns out to be failure. Or more accurately, the ability to cope with it by utilising *grit*.

Grit is the capacity to face failure point blank, learn from it, and try again. To fail repeatedly, fail hard, and keep on sucking it up. Duckworth explained. "Here's why. Learning is hard. True learning is fun, exhilarating and gratifying, but it's also daunting and exhausting. Educators and parents must first recognise that character is at least as important as intellect."

Duckworth examined the most successful students and found grit to be the core determinant of achievement. "Truly great accomplishment is not just about resisting temptations. It's about actively coping with the things that make you want to give up. It's the capacity for sustained effort in the face of setbacks."

Grit is the capacity to face failure point blank, learn from it, and try again.

Around the same time that Duckworth was publishing her work, the power of grit was also recognised just a few miles away in New York City. David Levin, co-founder of the pioneering KIPP schools programme, set out to help a network of American schools turn underprivileged children into high school graduates. Levin set high targets for his children, aiming for 75% of them to graduate with a college degree. Only a third of them actually reached this goal, but it wasn't the most 'intelligent' third. It was the individuals who committed to the struggle rather than opting for the 'easy win'.

Great Accomplishment is the capacity for sustained effort in the face of setbacks.

Growth

Players with grit tend to have a 'Growth Mindset'. Identified by Professor Carol Dweck, a 'Growth Mindset' offers a different understanding of achievement where a positive, healthy, mental attitude is engineered out of a 'solution-orientated' style of thinking. In her extraordinary ground-breaking book, *Mindset*, Dweck identifies a whole new psychology of success, examining the key ingredients required to make it to the top in sport, music, art, education, and business.

In a simple study, Dweck provided four-year-olds with a series of jigsaw puzzles to solve that got progressively harder. Once each child had solved one puzzle, they got to choose whether they repeated the same puzzle or moved onto the next one which was more complex and challenging. Some chose to repeat the same puzzle, and some chose to advance to the next stage. The question arose, therefore: why do you get differences in choice?

Even at this age, children with a growth mindset were showing a preference for struggle and challenge. They chose the harder puzzle to stretch, grow, and explore the boundaries of their ever-expanding potential.

Imagine players, who like these children, willingly choose more challenging tasks, always pursuing excellence, and eager to take on tougher challenges in order to improve. Contrast these players to those who only practice skills they can already do well. These players will always feel successful but don't give themselves a chance to develop.

The children who chose to repeat the simpler puzzle held a core belief that 'smart kids don't fail'. By sticking with the easier puzzle, these children avoided failure and the risk of being considered unintelligent.

Children with the growth mindset, on the other hand, believed that intelligence isn't something you either have or don't have, but something that you have to work for. They were revealing their beliefs about what success really is: the constant everyday battle of encountering challenges and overcoming difficulties in order to learn and improve.

So, does this mean that people with the growth mindset run the risk of encountering more failure? Absolutely. And that turns out to be 'where the magic happens'.

Here is the simple truth on how champions deal with the fear of failure:

- Winners hate to lose, but winners aren't afraid of losing.
- Champions dare to lose… in order to win.
- Courage is a choice, so is a Positive Winning Attitude.
- High achievers activate their Response-ABLE mindset. That is, they understand that the outcome doesn't define them; their response to try again does.
- Effort is valued more than outcome; with increased effort, the outcome improves.
- There is no significant achievement without significant failure.
- They realise they have three choices: give up, give in, or give it all they've got.
- Great athletes *cope*, the greatest athletes *embrace* pressure moments.

There is no fear or stress out there in the world; there are only people thinking fearfully, stressfully.

Wayne Dyer

Confidence

A culture of collaboration breeds confidence.

For a player to face failure over and over again and keep coming back takes confidence; a belief in their abilities, and a belief that with sustained effort they will succeed.

A striking example of the impact and power of self-belief and the effects that is can have on behaviour is evident in the realm of medicine. In the insightful book, *Change or Die*, by Alan Deutschman, the author reveals how 90% of patients who undergo coronary bypass or angioplasty surgery will not change their lifestyle even if their lives depend on it.

Edward Miller, MD, Dean of the medical school and Chief Executive Officer of the hospital at Johns Hopkins University, explains that such surgeries "are no more than temporary fixes," and that the patient's pain is relieved, but only for a while. Doctors tell their patients that they must "switch to a healthier lifestyle" if they want to keep the pain from coming back, avoid repeat surgery, and stop the disease before it kills them. Nevertheless, few change.

Dr. Miller explains, "If you look at people after coronary bypass grafting two years later, 90 percent of them have not changed their lifestyle." So it would seem that patients know they have a very bad disease and they know they should change their lifestyle, but for whatever reason, they can't or won't. The obvious question arises: why do patients not change their lifestyle even when faced with the ultimate consequence of death?

Even more astonishingly, people won't even keep regularly taking a pill (which has a good chance of saving their lives). In a study of 37,000 patients who were prescribed statins, nearly everyone took the pills for a month or two. By month three, about half had stopped. One year later, only one-third of patients were still taking the medicine which they were supposed to keep taking for the rest of their lives.

"Facts and fear do not work," explains Deutschman, no matter how rational the advice. Facts and fear won't sustain positive, lasting behavioural change. But why? Just how can healthcare provision post-surgery help patients to make life-altering changes in habit – and are initiatives created by leading physicians applicable to a soccer coach? Well, it's here that it starts to get interesting.

Deutschman articulates, very soundly, the success rate of a particular programme called 'The Ornish Approach' – where people do change for the long term. This is where we link back to self-belief and confidence in soccer, and how coaches can affect long-term change with their players. The real key is to give people *hope* and belief, not just facts. Use facts to set the scene and measure progress, but use hope and belief (leading to self-belief and confidence) to facilitate change. In traditional clinical research and medicine settings, patient compliance has an associated pessimistic value attached to it. In other words, physicians generally hold a low level of regard for patients subscribing totally to their post-treatment regimes. Deutschman writes, "The doctors remind you that you've got to start living in a healthier way," but "they really don't *believe* you can change. Their lack of conviction, betrayed by the look in their eyes or the tone of their voice or their body language, takes away from the impact of their words."

Convince-ability, it would seem, reveals itself as a significant factor above knowledge or experience; the ability to be *believable*.

Fitting, then, that research conducted by Dean Ornish, MD, and Professor of Medicine at the University of California at San Francisco, finds improved patient treatment adherence levels through a different approach. After a series of successful trials in the late 1970s, Ornish and his colleagues (in 1993) identified 333 patients who suffered from "severely clogged arteries" and had qualified for bypass or angioplasty surgery. In many of these cases, patients were suffering from crippling disease and needed instant relief. The Ornish group persuaded 194 of them to forego surgery (practically guaranteeing immediate relief but only a 'sticking plaster' solution) and try lifestyle change instead.

The entire team of professionals in the Ornish camp was made up of a nutritionist, cardiologist, psychologist, yoga teacher, chef, and meditation instructor. The team was assembled to take a whole new holistic approach to behavioural change. The team worked closely with the patients to help them quit smoking and switch to an extreme vegetarian diet. The patients came together and met twice a week for group conversations as well as engaging in yoga classes, meditation sessions, relaxation routines, and aerobic exercise – all designed to form a new daily routine and form new habits.

After one full year of being involved in this programme, patients were discharged and were left on their own, to fend for themselves. After being subjected to the radical new approach for 12 months straight, the real test was to see how many patients would continue their new healthy living lifestyle in the absence of the support mechanisms offered by the Ornish team.

Naturally, some people predicted a very low adherence level to the new regime, possibly due to findings from other studies. Indeed, most patients were predicted to drop out before the end of the first year. But, despite these doubts offered by 'conventional wisdom', nearly three years after the rigorous intervention, 77 percent of the patients had stuck with the lifestyle changes and safely avoided the need for heart surgery. They had stopped or, in many cases, reversed the progress of their disease.

So, what exactly was it that allowed Team Ornish to completely reverse the odds and inspire almost 80% of patients to radically change their lives forever? In revealing the answer, Dr. Ornish invites us to connect with the real truth behind positive and lasting behavioural change. He explains that the team took the time to give the patients *hope*, make them *believe* in themselves, and *convince* them that they could change.

They helped their patients learn and practice new habits and skills whilst encouraging them to think differently about themselves and their conditions. In more traditional medical practice, the recovery strategy post-surgery is almost completely reliant upon the doctor telling the patient that they *must* change, whilst all the while *failing to believe(!)* that they actually can and will.

And, because the doctor doesn't believe the patient can change, the patients both absorb and reflect this belief. Thus, an entire dependency on the only perceived cure – a cocktail of drugs and surgery – is formed.

But what are the actual results of this holistic lifestyle approach? Without actual objective measurement, how do we really know this approach works? Well, actually, here's where it gets very exciting. In all of the Ornish trials, the frequency of chest pains fell by 90% after the first month. This rapid and immediate improvement acted as a powerful motivator for the patients who were engaged with the programme. Even though it was a very tough and demanding one, the patients felt and saw immediate change. Motivated by early success, and a full year of comprehensive and unconditional support from the Ornish team, the patients became instilled with the understanding and belief necessary to continue on their own. 'Self-regulation' – the ability to practice independently of the professional team – was achieved.

Clearly, we could replace patients with players, health with performance, and surgeon with soccer coach. In a modern day coaching world, where statistical data saturates tactical evaluation, and technical strategies are highly prioritised, coaches must remember that at the heart of coaching lies the human element. And that they should not forsake the 'art' in favour of the 'science'.

Coaches who take the time to give their players *hope*, empower them to *believe* in themselves, and positively persuade them (especially during tough times), end up inspiring progress over the long-term.

A great story relating to this was during my time working with the U18 Birmingham City FC team in the second leg away tie against Liverpool at Anfield.

After a convincing 0-3 home defeat at St. Andrews, two weeks before, we travelled north in an attempt to recover the tie. Just 12 minutes into the game, we conceded another goal, taking the tie to 0-4. In a difficult and seemingly hopeless situation, captain Ashley Sammons found himself on the edge of the box in the 43rd minute with no option to pass forward. With only a second to think, he struck the ball right-footed from 30 yards, sending it looping into the top right-hand corner, live on national TV, to equalise for half-time 1-1. Even though Liverpool beat us that night, in the post-match interview Ashley explained what was going through his mind: "I've been working mentally with my coaches to not accept any limits that people try to place on me." Ashley knew that the only limits that exist are the ones we place on ourselves.

In a match-defining moment, Ashley continued to believe when others did not. Because of this, he was rewarded with his first-team senior debut away at Sunderland's Stadium of Light under then manager Alex Mcleish. Ashley, now player-turned-coach, continues to spread the same hope, belief, and inspiration to his young players today.

Self-Worth

Self-worth is a player's most important possession: it's knowing our personal value to the world regardless of any situation or circumstance we may face. Whatever happens, I'm a good person with a good heart and good intentions. And that's the crux of the problem. In a world where ad campaigns tell youngsters they must 'eat, drink, and breathe football' to have any chance at success, it is no surprise many players entwine their whole identities with soccer. They hang their self-worth on how good they think, or how good they perceive others think, their abilities are as a footballer. Rightly or wrongly, they put themselves at risk of the following thought pattern: 'If I'm not a good player, then I am worthless'. The motivational and emotional consequences of such thinking can be dire. No wonder these players fear failure.

Developing a Response-*ABLE* Mindset

Welcoming failure as an opportunity to learn is a key ingredient for success and players need help to overcome any fears they hold about underperforming. We know being fearful of failure can inhibit performance, but this knowledge is not enough to help players to shake this fear and welcome failure. As coaches, how we interact with players, what is reinforced, what is ignored, and how we evaluate them, can help strengthen a more Response-*ABLE* mindset. This is seen no more than in Messi's early experiences in football.

The 'secret' to Lionel Messi's Success

It would be easy to think that Messi was born with a God-given talent. There's no doubt in my mind that Lionel Messi is the best footballer in the world. Records such as 91 goals within a calendar year in 2011-2012, or a record-breaking five FIFA Ballon d'Or World Player of the Year awards speak for themselves.

In 2011, I was fortunate enough to spend time at La Masia. "What's his secret?" I asked Lionel's youth team educational mentor, Ruben Bonastre, who nurtured Xavi, Iniesta, Fabregas and the great Puyol amongst others. "Well," Ruben said, glancing at me with a warm smile, as if to forgive my naivety, "when Lionel was younger he was physically smaller than most of the other boys. He used to run with the ball all of the time. And his coaches realised that he used to always lose the ball whenever he ran with it. So they had a choice. They could either tell him to play it safe, keep the ball, don't give it away, keep it simple, or they could choose a different message."

They chose something different, and this very decision may have been one of the key factors in the success of Messi. Instead of telling him to play safe, they played him down an age group so he played against players who were physically the same size. And crucially they didn't criticise his efforts to dribble and beat players with the ball. The coaches recognised he had a genuine, sincere, burning passion for this part of the game. So they decided that every time he ran with the ball and lost it, they would stop the practice, ask him if he could think of a way of doing it better, and provided another opportunity to try again. *Stop, here, have the ball again, and this time try dropping the shoulder or try pushing inside out with the laces.*

Why is this story significant to us? What does a child learn growing up in this type of environment? Messi learned a fundamental and life-changing principle from the process the coaches chose to pursue. He was not going to be defined simply by the outcome of his performance. His coaches were rewarding effort over 'talent' by actively praising his endeavour rather than his outcome. What did Messi learn from this? He learned that he should have no fear of making mistakes because the 'mistake' was not going to define his progress.

- My coaches aren't going to define me by the mistakes I make.
- It's my effort, persistence, and ability to respond to setbacks that counts.
- Failure is temporary and necessary on the journey to being world class.
- My effort to improve is rated more than the 'natural talent' I believe I have.

Like Messi's earliest experiences, we can help players develop a Response-*ABLE* mindset through small changes in the way we work with them.

Re-Defining Success (and Failure)

Matthew Syed's compelling book, *Bounce – How Champions are Made*, uncovers some poignant examples of performance excellence. One of the studies presented looks at figure skaters and, in particular, the difference between the number of mistakes made in training between elite skaters and amateurs. The results revealed that the elite group made, on average, five times more mistakes than their amateur peers.

At first glance, the natural assumption would be that the amateurs would make more mistakes in training. But the study actually revealed that the routines of the elite skaters were becoming increasingly more difficult. Each time the elite practiced, they pushed themselves outside their comfort zone and ran the risk of failing in the process. They lived by the principle that the more times they failed, the closer they got to mastering their new routines.

> **You miss 100% of the shots you don't take.**
>
> Wayne Gretzky

Great coaches recognise that players and teams can succeed even when they fail. People succeed when they are able to push through adverse conditions and remain committed to the cause regardless of the outcome. By definition, this is one of the most important ingredients in helping players and teams overcome the fear of failure. When coaches help their players to focus on a performance process – as opposed to merely an outcome – they learn to measure their 'success' as a *journey*, not a destination. Subtle difference, big thought change. It means that as a player I might lose the game, but the most important thing is not always the result, it's the process of improving my performance. It's about asking the question: am I a better version of myself today compared with yesterday? Even when we 'lose' we may have, in fact, won. The result may be in our favour but if our performance wasn't as good as it could have been, then it's not a true win. Elite performance is not achieved by the absence of apprehension, it is achieved through the mental capacity to harness it. Elite performers do not achieve greatness because they do not experience fear and anxiety. They simply develop their abilities to overcome it.

Here's the interesting thing. Gold medal mindsets do not see 'pressure' as a problem, they perceive it as a privilege. They understand and recognise these moments as significant opportunities to grow, learn, and improve. They know that without these moments, they would never be able to practice being at their very best when it matters the most. They know it's not about performing perfectly every single time; it's about effort.

Great effort reflects great attitude, attitude is a choice, and champions choose wisely.

When the choice is made every single day to maximise effort in training and in competition, positive change starts to occur. This is where personal transformation starts. 'Success' then is not a momentary outcome, but an attitude of perseverance and endeavour. A commitment to constant and never-ending improvement.

If we measure success merely by an undesired outcome (like losing the match or failing to make the time in a sprint) – a one-time judgement – then it is true that we may have failed. If, on the other hand, you measure success differently, then there's a deeper lesson to be learned. If you believe that success is the capacity for sustained effort in the face of setbacks, a willingness to respond to difficulty in adverse conditions, trying again even when there's no obvious signal of immediate triumph, then you'll find a different perspective. You'll find a more enduring measurement of lasting success.

Here's why.

Coaches and teams who see short-term failure as a predictor of future potential take fewer risks in order to avoid the perceived pain of failure. They are more likely to believe people will judge their failure as an indicator of limited ability or a sign of missing talent. In an attempt to protect themselves from appearing vulnerable, they will go to great lengths to prevent future failure. It is only when we realise and accept failure as a friend who offers feedback that we give ourselves a chance to learn, grow, and improve as a result. Those who achieve more in the end are the ones who have failed the most on the way. This is as true in sport as it is in life.

Call it what you will. Some call it spirit or character, others positive mental attitude. What is certain, though, is that the defining qualities of empowered thinkers, doers, and achievers is not to be found in the easily observable outcomes of one-off competition or short-term success. These qualities reveal themselves in performers during moments when it makes no sense to keep going and all seems lost; yet they keep going with energy, hope, endeavour, resilience, and discipline. The choice to continue on the path of constant and never-ending improvement is made. It is very difficult to beat someone who refuses to give up because, when all else is equal, talent comes second to character. An athlete's talent and ability may get them to the front door, but it will be their character that defines their potential in the end.

Remember the KIPP schools programme that found how students with grit were much more likely to graduate with a college degree than those children who lacked grit? In an attempt to communicate the importance of 'grit' as a life-long ingredient, the programme's founder – David Levin – shifted the focus of development training for every teacher in KIPP. All teachers were encouraged to infuse a very simple but powerful message into their teaching. Failure was to be embraced as an opportunity to demonstrate how tenaciously students could overcome it, and sport became a central vehicle for conveying this key message. Instead of a low grade in an exam, for example, being perceived as a permanent negative outcome, teachers focused on the opportunity to overcome temporary failure.

What the KIPP programme so brilliantly proclaimed and embedded within the new educational philosophy was that failure was not 'final'. Each student, each person, would be measured by their effort levels rather than whether they achieved a certain grade. The message was simple: effort counts more than the result; effort matters more than the outcome. In approaching 'failure' this way, it's not only the perception of failure that changes, it's the whole emotional connection to what failure is and how it feels.

One of the most compelling principles on the high-performance journey is *how* and *what* coaches teach their athletes with regards to what success and failure *is*. Performers who think of success in terms of how much effort they invest in football, and failure as a learning opportunity rather than a defining outcome, respond better to the constant everyday challenges they are faced with, and they are more likely to carry on.

Hard-working, passionate, fearless coaches aspire to help their players *be more*. They challenge themselves constantly, pushing the boundaries of self-perceived limitation. They dare to be GREAT.

Create Certainty through Training

> **We don't perform under pressure;**
> **we sink to the level of our training.**
>
> Jason Fox

Ex-Royal Marine and SBS soldier, Jason Fox, encountered the ultimate fear of failure during a secret mission in a highly hostile location. In soccer, if you make a mistake, have a bad touch, or give the ball away, conceding a goal or losing a match is the consequence. In combat, the consequence of failure is probably death. That's why, in these extreme conditions – when bullets are flying, and the enemy is closing in – the

Special Forces live by a certain principle, a self-created secret affirmation.

That's why during training for highly volatile operations, marines plan for every eventuality. There is clarity in their plans which are then followed up with action as they are pushed beyond the point of exhaustion in their preparations. Through this, one of the finest fighting forces is able to perform under pressure, or sink to the level of their training. As a coach, this clarity infuses confidence. Having a crystal clear picture of exactly what you might face, then training and preparing purposefully, creates certainty... and certainty is the enemy of doubt. Coaching with certainty is coaching to overcome the fear of failure.

Controlling the Controllables

There are times in life when we cannot control the situations we find ourselves in, but we will always be able to control how we choose to respond. A Response-ABLE mind is a mind capable of selecting an empowered attitude in the most adverse of conditions. Choosing your attitude and approach to any given circumstance is *your choice*, and no one will ever be able to take that from you; no matter how hard things may get.

- Whatever situation you're in, you are always in control of your thoughts, beliefs, and attitudes.
- Choosing your response is within your control.
- There are multiple ways to respond to setbacks, challenges, and adversity.
- Champions choose their responses wisely.

Exercises

Signpost your Cultural Values, Beliefs, and Expectations *Together*.

Allow each person to be a contributing member of the exercise.

Creating a Culture Code

- What is most important to us?
- What do we stand for?
- What do we demand from each other?

Response examples may include *competitive toughness, resilience, honesty, discipline, enjoyment, togetherness, passion, perseverance.*

Split your complete team up into four or five groups, mixing staff and players together. Give each group a flip chart and allow 10-15 minutes for the groups to think and discuss their answers before writing them on the board and sharing them with the entire group. Ask two players or staff members to feedback and share with the room.

Circle the top three values the squad identified on each flip chart, using the exact words and phrases the team used to describe their values. Print them up for the dressing room and offices as an everyday reminder.

Shared Ownership – A Natural Way to Create Accountability

Meetings to establish clear expectations and non-negotiables for behaviour and performance, can be effective. Also, allowing the players and staff to share their ideas informally can sometimes be as beneficial. Not everything has to be categorised in a formal and rigid manner. The more natural the responses you can get, the better. These informal coaching moments may be walking from the training pitch collecting cones, or chats in the corridor. You can always write up appropriate thoughts and opinions into a simple and clear document for staff and players to sign and agree to later. Questions like, 'how can we improve?' or 'What do we need to do to keep improving our standards?' can act as prompts for people to express their thoughts and perspectives.

Specific actions

Define Success

...to your team of players and colleagues.

- Winning is doing the right thing, no matter what.
- Put effort into improving every day.
- Do your very best.
- Tackle your fears head on, stepping out of your comfort zone.
- Never give up; give it all you've got.
- Have a goal, a vision for yourself, and work every day to get there.

Re-define failure

Frame failure as a learning opportunity and experience, not a defining outcome of self-worth and identity. Some of the greatest achievements in life have been achieved by those who simply refused to give up.

Share Your Story

Every coach has a story. How did you fall in love with the game? Where did you learn to be a coach? What have some of your best memories been in coaching? What do you want to achieve in your coaching career? Why are you so passionate about being the coach of *this team*? Allowing the players to learn about you creates an expanded level of warmth and personal understanding which feeds a higher level of professional respect.

Instil Confidence

Create certainty through training. Share team session plans with the players ahead of training, walking them through the principles and purpose. Create individual athletic development training sessions scheduled to train, work, and 'live out' your principles of improvement. Ask the players to evaluate their own needs and co-create the framework for shared ownership and accountability.

Summary

Creating a culture for champions to flourish is about much more than writing a few words down on a flip chart and creating a poster for the wall. It involves careful consideration of the values, beliefs, and behaviours that will underpin and drive a successful winning environment.

More often than not, fear within a culture can derail positive momentum before you even begin; so, being a coach that can breed belief and empower players with resilience is critical. Coaches of the future will be leading players to develop their own levels of grit in order to grow, allowing space and time to respond to temporary setbacks, and appealing to effort and attitude over outcome. Truly great accomplishment, as we have discovered, is a lot more about how we respond when things go badly, and a lot less to do with how we cope when things go well. Success requires sustained effort, even if (and especially when) it gets tough.

PRINCIPLE 6
ESTABLISH ACCOUNTABILITY

Accountability is about people taking responsibility for their actions and behaviours. It underpins what a team stands for, what it believes in, and it drives success both on and off the pitch. Accountability reflects that no-one is bigger than the team. Timekeeping, extra practice, team meeting contributions, whatever it is – accountability helps take players and staff to the next level.

> **...when a defining moment comes along, you define the moment ... or the moment defines you.**
>
> Roy McAvoy, Tin Cup

Time Travel - The Cost of Ambition

Highly ambitious athletes possess a ruthless determination to succeed. In many ways, their drive to be the best becomes a healthy obsession. Every ounce of energy, every thought, indeed their entire being becomes possessed with the sole aim of high achievement. They live in a world where the margin for error is so small that the constant search for growth and development is magnified and continuous.

Every performance, every training session, every detail is analysed, monitored, and evaluated individually and by an army of sports scientists, coaches, and analysts as their game becomes more professional. No wonder, then, that one of the pitfalls of this incessant journey is a mind that shoots forwards and backwards in time. A mind that recalls both previous successes and failures, and one that becomes unable to predict future outcomes before they take place.

Lurking behind this train of thought are a few fundamental flaws. Is active reflection a positive behaviour? Absolutely. The ability to think back over recent events, in detail, to learn and move forward is, in fact, a necessity. The danger in this process, however, is the distraction from the present moment. You get caught up thinking about the past, then flicking forwards into the future. I've seen this happen with countless performers over the years and leads to what sport psychologists call 'Paralysis through Analysis'. Or, more simply, *overthinking*. At first glance, this sounds quite absurd and possibly plain contradictory. Surely the more thought that someone puts into performance, the better? Well, yes, but only to a point. Overthinking can literally lead to a self-imposed paralysed state, where action is replaced with hesitation and anxiety.

Here's an example from the sporting world, one that is now infamous amongst golf enthusiasts around the world.

On Sunday, April 14th 1996, at the Augusta National Golf Club, an unprecedented Masters meltdown was about to unfold. Australian-born Greg Norman was six strokes clear of his closest challenger, Nick Faldo. To all who understand and follow golf, this kind of lead going into the final day of the tournament should have signified an inevitable championship victory for Norman. He was out of sight and anticipated by all to play out the round, as a formality, and be crowned Masters Champion. Instead, in an epic psychological meltdown, the 41-year-old shot a final round of 78 falling to a five-stroke loss to Faldo in a jaw-dropping 11 shot turnaround.

Now referred to as one of the greatest 'chokes' in golfing history, the 1996 Augusta final day asks a very important question for both athletes and coaches. *What was it* that led to such a destructive breakdown in performance? After all, Norman was at the top of his game. Turning pro in 1986, he had held the world number 1 ranking for a remarkable 331 weeks and finished his pro career with 90 titles worldwide. What exactly went through Norman's mind that day to affect the outcome so drastically? In an Australian TV interview conducted after the competition, Norman revealed that he lost focus, and experienced uncontrollable thoughts. He explained, "If you've got garbage in your head, you can't be focused on the mission you want to achieve." Critically, under extreme pressure, we know that perception narrows and we lose track of time. Overthinking can cause an increase in doubt and apprehension. In high-pressure moments, when athletes can get anxious about performing, they can overanalyse and overthink; these processes sabotage their physical performances.

Examples from across sport offer sufficient proof that the mental and emotional processes an individual (or team) goes through can be the defining elements of competition when the margins for error are so small.

Pia Nilsson along with Lynn Marriot, coaches who have worked with former world number 1 golfers like Annika Sorenstam and Yani Tseng, offer a simple but brilliant insight. They highlight that most athletes' performance states can change under 'pressure'. Critically though, the athletes who best cope and respond, are the ones who *best understand how pressure can affect them personally.*

With a heightened level of self-understanding, tailored mental strategies can be adopted. Although simple, this makes perfect sense. After all, if I'm an athlete whose mind begins to race uncontrollably, I know I may need to breathe to stay focused, or centre my attention on a pre-performance routine to remain calm. I know that I am accountable for my performance and that my actions demonstrate my accountability. Staying in the moment – undistracted and present – is an ultimate skill that allows golfers to centre their attention on one task at a time.

Returning to the Greg Norman story, further insight is offered by neuroscientists and psychologists.

Sian Beilock, Psychology President of Barnard College, and author of *Choke*, has studied golfers comprehensively. Beilock points out that misdirected thinking can inhibit performance by distracting athletes from 'task-relevant' actions. Once the mind becomes distracted (through focusing on 'other things'), it can spiral out of control, causing the brain to concentrate on less important information in the environment, spending mental energy in the wrong direction.

But that's not the only challenge for golfers. Neuroscientists have discovered that the golfer's brain behaves very differently in high-pressure situations. By placing electrode-fitted caps on golfers' temporal lobes, designed to ascertain which parts of the brain are active at certain times, the amygdala (also known in popular psychology as the fear centre) has been shown to become overactive causing a heightened state of anxiety. We now know, that in those crucial moments in the spotlight of the Augusta 1986 championships, Greg Norman *choked;* and it was all down to what was going on in his mind.

It's true that the ability to think back over recent events (in detail), to learn, and to move forward is necessary for growth and development. However, the ability not to get stuck in the past, or fast forward into the future, is what defines present moment focus.

As the best-selling author Eckhart Tolle puts it in the powerful book *Stillness Speaks*, "The past only exists in a memory of the now. The future when it gets here will be in the present." The only real moment that exists is now, the rest is merely a mental illusion. Present moment focus is the ability to centre your attention on the now. This moment.

The past is for learning from, not living in

Champion athletes remain focused in the present moment effortlessly and automatically when required. In 'The Zone', time slows down, opponents become predictable and easy to read, and movements become fluent and coherent. Typified by low levels of thought, it is here – in The Zone – that the subconscious mind takes over and the elite brain kicks into play. The clearer and more focused you are in your mind of what you want to achieve in the moment, the more likely you will achieve it. As we know, what you focus on – you get more of.

> **The mind is like a parachute; it doesn't work if it isn't open.**
>
> Frank Zappa

Former Rugby Superstar Johnny Wilkinson has attributed that it was this tenacity for practice that led to his famous 2003 World Cup-winning drop goal against Australia in the last minute of extra time. The countless hours of practice had prepared him for his moment of greatness.

Practice that included not just physical, technical, and tactical elements – but which included the psychological too. A type of mental rehearsal to train his brain on the field of practice. Wilkinson believed that it was possible to practice in the mind to stay focused, high in concentration, and in the moment. As an elite performer, he was passionate about reducing errors, leaving nothing to chance, improving 1%, and gaining that competitive edge.

Dave Alred, Johnny's kicking coach, who began working with him when Wilkinson was 16 was impressed from the start, not for his physical qualities but by the courage he had to think differently and explore new techniques during practice. One of these techniques included centring his energy on a central point in his body before kicking, and visualising a line connecting the ball and the centre point of the goal posts. Johnny Wilkinson had the capacity to play with ideas before rejecting them. He kept his mind open and considered new approaches to training.

Wilkinson also disagrees with people who say that sometimes you'll have good days and sometimes bad days. "I believe that we create the good days and we create the bad days," he says.

Most people say they want different and better results in their work, but they're not courageous enough to think and act differently. Johnny Wilkinson would practice his kicking for hour upon hour, tuning every fine detail until he could execute his skills exactly as he wanted to. He took responsibility for his performances and trained because he knew he would be accountable at key moments. At one practice session, he remembers taking six hours to complete just six successful kicks to the standard he was happy with. After training, he would ask himself, "If I had to take this kick to win the match, could I pull it off?"

It is this healthy obsession for excellence that underpins all great performers.

It's no surprise, then, that having practiced so diligently – blocking out all levels of distraction and remaining completely focused in the moment – Johnny was able to perform at his peak level when it mattered.

Johnny Wilkinson teaches us:

- We create the good days through the quality of our thoughts about those days.
- Preparing for an opportunity is better than an opportunity arising and not being prepared.
- Great moments are born from great opportunities.
- To achieve extraordinary results, we must be brave enough to think differently.
- Great performers all have healthy obsessions for constant and never-ending improvement.

In the same fashion, David Beckham was completely present in the moment when he stepped up to take a last-gasp free kick against Greece in a 2002 World Cup Qualifying match at Old Trafford. After taking several free kicks in the game, each narrowly missing the target, the team may have exited the automatic qualification stages if he didn't score with what looked to be England's final chance in the 93rd minute of the match.

Trailing 1-2 to Greece, England were awarded a free kick on the right-hand side of Greece's penalty area. Both Paul Scholes and Teddy Sheringham stepped up to the ball as contenders to take the kick. But Beckham, ruthlessly persistent with unshakable determination and belief, waved them away.

In that moment, Beckham can be seen taking deep breaths, slowly placing the ball on the ground, and stepping into his pre-performance routine. Visualising the ball floating over the wall into the net whilst breathing deeply and focusing his thoughts; he blocked out the crowd, shut out the pressure, and executed the perfect free-kick high into the top left-hand corner. In that moment, he became a hero. But that moment was only possible because of the thousands of hours he had spent practicing the kick over and over again behind the scenes. The countless repetitions and corrections he carried out in practice became crucial.

Both Wilkinson and Beckham demonstrated how a process of conscious rehearsal and improvement on the training pitch enabled them to enter a sub-conscious state of mind – which allowed them to perform at their best – when it mattered most.

> **I know of no more encouraging fact than the unquestionable ability of man to elevate his life by a conscious endeavour.**
>
> Henry David Thoreau

A deeper look at these two athletes reveals some similarities. Both had individual qualities of internal drive and motivation to be the best. Both practiced intensely. Without doubt, huge credit is due to both men for the consistency and intrinsic discipline they applied on their respective fields of play. But, we also see how the environment at both Manchester United FC and England Rugby fostered and supported those qualities to grow and develop.

The cultural leaders at the time, in Sir Alex Ferguson and Sir Clive Woodward, intentionally created mindsets that were attuned to rewarding effort and establishing accountability. In a sense, establishing an environment of accountability is like ensuring the right temperature in the swimming pool for a swimmer. No matter how gifted or talented the swimmer, if the water is freezing cold then the conditions prevent best practice.

As a coach, it is your responsibility to provide an environment that creates accountability within your team. That accountability will drive individuals to improve, learn, grow, and improve.

Specific actions

Create a Player-Led Individual Athletic Development Plan

In Principle 1, we examined the value of measuring, managing, and monitoring specific traits required to succeed in each position. We looked at a *Player Performance Profile* to scrutinise (and log) a number of key areas, which then formed the basis of an improvement plan. Here, the Athletic Development Plan is a continuation of that approach, and focuses on a particular process for improvement.

Players become accountable when they feel they are consciously working towards specific, meaningful goals. To reiterate from earlier, these goals can be easily identified, recorded, and measured based on the position each player has. When you create an individual athletic development plan, you are offering guidance and direction in addition to a feeling of purposeful significance.

- Break down 2-3 areas in each category of mental, technical, tactical, physical skills and traits, and agree a plan of action for the next two week period.
- At the end of two weeks, schedule a one-to-one 'drop-in' session and ask each player to feedback on their progress.
- Make it clear that each player has sole responsibility and freedom to create and drive their own programme.

Here's a simple and genuine example of a position-specific development analysis for a Premier League central midfield player I worked with. In this analysis, the player identified certain areas for improvement – forward-placed penetrating passes, and positions higher up the pitch – and wanted to know the specific percentages relating to his ability to play them in a match (which the analyst provided). From this measurement, he developed a plan to work very specifically on a technical-mental goal, as a two-week focus.

Technical and Tactical	Play forward, penetrating passes that break lines and create attacking chances.	
	Play forwards from the middle and attacking third by picking up positions higher up the pitch.	
Mental	Have the confidence to risk passes in order to create goals for the team.	
	Respond positively if I give the ball away in attempting a forward pass. "Re-set, recover, re-focus."	
	Be brave to try again with the next pass. Keep taking risks in the middle and attacking third!	
Statistical Measurement	**Successful Passes**	**Unsuccessful Passes**
	66% of passes were square and backwards.	72% intercepted from middle and attacking third.
	34% of passes were forward.	60% were forwards, 12% sideways and backwards.
	20% broke the lines from the middle to attacking third.	18% misplaced (given away).
	1 assist – leading to the only goal of the game.	

In the basic table above, 66% of successful passes were square and backwards. At first glance, it would seem that the player was safe with his passing. On closer examination, however, 72% of unsuccessful passes were attempted from the middle and attacking third with one assist leading to the only goal of the game. This central midfield player lost the ball a lot, but lost it while attempting to play forwards and create chances in tight situations.

Statistically (in this match) he was attempting incredibly difficult passes in tight situations to gain an attacking advantage. Psychologically, these statistics gave the coaches an insight into the player's mentality. He was, in fact, being brave enough to try the difficult passes with confidence, despite the setbacks and misplaced passes. This type of attitude in this game could have been the reason why he made the only successful assist leading to the team's narrow 1-0 victory – a great example of mindset in action.

The Drive to Succeed

In May 1954, Roger Bannister ran a mile in under four minutes for the first time in history. Reports of his astonishing 3 minutes 59.4-second feat flashed around the world. For many years previously, scientists and doctors proclaimed the impossibility of such a feat, stating that the human heart would never be able to take the strain of such intensity. Muscles would tear, and bones fracture under such stress; such a performance was simply unfeasible. But on this day in 1954, Roger Bannister decided to kick out the commonly-held belief that it wasn't possible and chose to focus on his goal, choosing a more empowered belief.

What happened immediately after Bannister's achievement is as exciting as the first part of this story. As the news broke in the weeks and months following his great achievement, runners from around the world started to come forward reporting their similar achievements over the same distance. Within seven months, 37 runners had also succeeded in breaking the four-minute mile. Within three years, 300 more did it. What exactly was going on here? Had we accelerated our physical training programmes creating a rapidly-improved human physiology? I don't think so. What happened was a significant shift in the beliefs that people held about what was possible and what was not. One man endeavoured to beat 'well informed' odds, and in doing so, paved the way for others to believe in the possible. All 300 runners were capable of achieving what Bannister achieved, but he was unlimited in the way he thought and believed.

> **Those who say it can't be done, shouldn't get in the way of those who are doing it.**
>
> George Bernard Shaw

Had Bannister failed in his earlier attempts to achieve this goal? Absolutely! But once again, he wasn't going to be defined by his previously unsuccessful attempts. In fact, it was the opposite. Every time he failed, he believed he was learning something more valuable. He saw each disappointment as a chance to get better, to run faster, and in doing so he cultivated a champion's mentality:

"I prepared myself very carefully in a careful and concentrated fashion. I tried to establish this now or never attitude, because I knew that unless I was successful in attaining this attitude I would perhaps lose my chance by letting myself fall prey to the mental reaction so common to athletes

– that is thinking that there would always be a next time of deciding, perhaps that is not the day."

The underlying common denominator appears again and again. But, the key to all these great success stories is not merely an exposure to failure. That's only part one of the story. We all face setbacks, we all struggle, and we all (at times) fail. If it were merely the exposure to failure that causes transformative success, wouldn't we all be outstanding achievers? In the classic, award-winning, *Man's Search for Meaning*, Viktor Frankl best articulates the power of belief by sharing his experiences as a prisoner at Auschwitz concentration camp:

"We who lived in concentration camps can remember the men who walked through the huts comforting others, giving away their last piece of bread. They may have been few in number, but they offer sufficient proof that everything can be taken from a man but one thing: the last of the human freedoms - to choose one's attitude in any given set of circumstances, to choose one's own way. The way in which a man accepts his fate and all the suffering it entails, the way in which he takes up his cross, gives him ample opportunity, even in the most difficult circumstances, to add a deeper meaning to his life."

The Response-Able Mindset

The next part of this chapter's story is as important as the first.

Being exposed to failure is step one. Step two is choosing your response mode. And a person's response mode is inherently linked to accountability.

Experiencing failure must be accompanied by an inner voice of resilience; a perception of being able to advance and being able to cope to 'get by'. This is where (for high achievers) the focus shifts. Instead of internally accepting they are just a consequence of circumstance, they recognise and focus on their ability to respond. They embrace and simultaneously transcend failure, by *perceiving* it as an opportunity to demonstrate how tenaciously they can overcome the challenge. In the depths of their darkness, they answer a very simple question: *am I a victim or am I a fighter?* And, in answering this very question ("I am a fighter"), they not only reveal their own hidden depths of resilience, they simultaneously choose a path to a far more fulfilling future.

Those who pursue the end goal with such persistence encounter a simple truth: in the end, there are actually no limitations. The only limitations that exist are the ones we create for ourselves through the way that we think. And if limitations are created from thoughts, we are therefore in control to remove them. This is why, in the end, attitude not only drives performance but defines it – at the very highest level, under the most demanding conditions.

Fighting Fit

> **We cannot always control the situations we find ourselves in, but we can always control our response.**
>
> Viktor Frankl

Jordon Mutch heard the news loud and clear.

Nine months of full rehab, sleeping in an oxygen tent for two months, and wheelchair treatment for two weeks. Now, more than ever before, he was going to be tested. Victim or fighter? The choice was his, and his alone.

No-one prepares players for moments like these. Yet, it is these very moments that contain the potential to define a whole year, a career, a lifetime. In many respects, it's a player's worst nightmare. To have to hear that you're not going to be able to lead and live the life you have loved for so long. And the thought process is nearly always the same.

The shock of the initial news turns into denial and rejection; *this isn't happening, not to me.* After a while the anger shifts to acceptance followed by the realisation of knowing *I'm going to have to face this.*

There was only one thing that didn't quite make sense to me when working with Jordon. One thing I could never quite fathom. He had an emotional detachment to him that I hadn't come across before. An unfazed persona. After success, he would never be the one bouncing off the walls. Nor would he be falling through the floor after big and sometimes unexpected defeats. He had an inherent ability to find emotional stability.

It is something that I would later learn that all top performers need to have. They either learn it early in life, or they develop it later on; either way, in the end, I am certain they all have it.

It's a quality which enables them to detach themselves emotionally from both the complexity of the circumstance and the sideshow surrounding the result. An emotionally detached clinical focus is also a quality which sharpens the athletic brain. In the defining moments – when a match is won or lost – elite athletes combine competitive fire with ice-cold clinical thinking. Emotional detachment is the quality that creates an ability to think clearly under pressure, stay composed in the face of extreme adversity, and find solutions faster than most during difficult and challenging situations.

Without doubt, this psychological ingredient enabled Jordon to return one year later to the field of play more focused and hungrier than ever.

Here are three lessons that Jordon learned through his injury;

1. **Control the Controllables.** Don't let what you can't do get in the way of what you can do at the time. Turn your attention to strengthening your upper body, or studying the best players in the game. Focus your attention on what you are in control of.
2. **Physical injury does not have to mean psychological injury.** Stay as committed to the training programme as ever. Set simple goals and stick to them.
3. **Use the time wisely.** Focus on the player you are becoming; better every day.

Jordon can now be found competing in the Premier League where he plays week in week out.

Here are some common challenges and potential solutions when working to support players through injury.

Seven common challenges athletes face during injury.

1. **Mental Fatigue.** Both athletes and staff become tired with ongoing, never-ending rehabilitation, and return to a training schedule. Boredom sets in, complacency manifests.
2. **Self-Doubt and Uncertainty.** In this difficult time, confidence can drop; there's an unpredictable element to the recovery process because no-one is sure what the final outcome will be.
3. **Existential Threat.** The pain and suffering regarding a player's career potential, reputation, and future aspirations are now in focus.
4. **Damage versus Loss of Identity.** "Who am I if I can't play now?" If I am what I do... then what am I if I don't?
5. **Emotional Frustration. (Idealization-Frustration-Demoralization)** A growing sense of built-up tension, anger, and frustration leading to negative behaviour.
6. **Social Isolation.** A tendency for athletes to remove themselves from the team environment, choosing to avoid interaction.
7. **Avoidance / Denial.** The refusal to accept the situation as it is.

Seven key steps to improve the injury process for athletes

1. **Accurate Framing.** Seeing the situation as it is, not better, not worse. Assessing the accuracy of the circumstance.
2. **Setting Expectations.** Painting a crystal-clear picture of the exact time frame, process, and journey of the next however many months.
3. **Connective Feedback.** Involving senior management teams in medical updates to prevent result-based praise.
4. **Super Strengths.** Finding out what an athlete can work on physically that won't harm the injury.
5. **Energy Tank.** Fuel the energy tank. Go to the places, listen to the music, and surround oneself with the people they love.
6. **Support Networks.** Involve the athletes in training scenarios socially. Encourage injured players to give feedback in analysis sessions and work out in the gym around the other players if they wish to.
7. **Individual Needs.** Know who the right person is to connect with them. Physio, Psychologist, Coach, Analyst, Kit man.

Constant and Never-ending Improvement

Remaining separate from the outcome and emotionally detached doesn't mean athletes don't care. Far from it. It's because they care that distance is fundamental. It prevents them getting caught up in a web of unnecessary thought. One way athletes prevent this from happening is by focusing on the process of improvement rather than just the outcome.

"Who are the very best players you've ever worked with and why?"

This was the question I posed to Steve Clarke, former manager of West Bromwich Albion when sitting in the manager's office one afternoon after training. He explained that two of the best players he's ever worked with (Steven Gerrard and Frank Lampard), had two common characteristics.

1. They were the hardest workers.
2. They had a healthy obsession and constantly looked to improve. They were never satisfied, always searching for the smallest margins and details to get better.

It is a classic trait of the champion athlete. The greats like Gerrard, Lampard, Messi, Ronaldo, and so on, are all different in so many ways yet the same when it comes to a relentless search for improvement. A winning attitude that is undeterred by temporary outcomes of success or defeat. An ability to rise above the noise of current circumstance and focus to fine-tune the process of their own progress. It's something striker and Belgium International Romelu Lukaku told me in a changing room one day after training. He believed it to be the very reason behind his goal-scoring spree that season, at West Brom, whilst on loan from Chelsea. "When I was young, training at Chelsea, I looked up to Nicolas Anelka and Didier Drogba. People would say to me you're going to be the next Anelka or the next Drogba and I would always stop them to say no. I'm going to be me, Romelu Lukaku. Every day I work harder, training extra when everyone has gone home. This is why I believe I have scored goals. My attitude is to always get better. Never settle for less than my best."

Clarke, Lukaku, Gerrard, Lampard. Each sharing a similar perspective. Separate from the outcome, fixed on the process of never-ending improvement. They owned their performances. They were accountable.

Rewarding Attitude over Ability – A Coach's Imperative

Former Premier League defender and current Assistant Manager of Arsenal, Steve Bould, was the youth manager of the U18's Arsenal team before his rise to the senior men's side. He explained that on occasions he would pick the hardest-working players for matches regardless of the potential for defeat. In this way, he said, "rewarding effort and attitude with a place in the team clearly sends out a message about how important attitude really is."

Bill Beswick, international Sports Psychologist, further explained the importance of attitude for players. Players with great attitudes and an abundance of talent will make it to the highest level. Players with talent but a poor attitude may occasionally flatter to deceive but will, ultimately, never realise their full potential. Athletes lower in talent but with excellent attitudes maximise every opportunity and eventually are rewarded with success, if not in sport then certainly in their lives. Bill was the first person to share with me the famous quote from Tim Notke, "Hard work beats talent when talent doesn't work hard."

Genius is 1% inspiration and 99% perspiration.

Thomas Edison

Specific actions for establishing accountability

Create opportunities for players to drive their own programme and training plan, and record progress.

Define the word "accountability" in the language that players best understand and refer to it often. E.g., "We own our success and failure. We win together, we lose together."

Demonstrate accountability yourself as the coach in your working day, in practice, living out the value itself in what you DO rather than what you say.

Always provide opportunities for players to do extra training with coaches and staff.

Be available to work *with* (and alongside) players allowing them to take ownership and accountability for their own progress.

Provide roles and responsibilities for players to fulfil for the team and rotate leadership duties; e.g., preparing the table for meal times, collecting the kit and equipment, leading a player meeting, making the teas at lunchtime, carrying the drinks bottles, leading the warm-up.

Summary

Attitude not only drives performance but defines it, at the very highest level, under the most demanding conditions. And attitude underpins accountability.

There are many variables that can shape the landscape of elite performance. As the technological advances in modern-day competitive arenas unfold, so must the capacity to embrace and capitalise on these advantages. Data-driven statistical analysis can reveal objective patterns that subjective opinion struggles to observe. Then there are the coded performance analysis software packages, driven to enhance our evaluative capabilities and decision-making processes. Elite performance environments are, without doubt, tasked to search out the 1% marginal improvement gains that can, when accumulated, create a clear competitive advantage.

The *undeniable* truth, however, is that on the greatest stage, tracing the biographical histories of the most successful achievers, it is not 'talent' but attitude that counts the most! Creating an environment where players are accountable to themselves and the team through shared ownership is a clear competitive edge in the modern day.

PRINCIPLE 7
EXPLAIN YOUR STYLE OF PLAY

> I keep six honest serving men (They taught me all I knew).
> Their names are What and Why and When and How
> and Where and Who.
>
> Rudyard Kipling, The Elephant's Child

In Principle 5, we established how clarity breeds confidence.

Making sure each player knows what is expected of them, how to play, and what to do, boosts certainty. If they are crystal clear on exactly what you are asking them to do, they will be supremely confident in delivering the action plan you want to carry out.

Doubt is the enemy of confidence.

Clarity is the key to creating confident players.

A clear style of play, coaching philosophy, and game plan – which articulate specific objectives, strategy, and tactics – is a coach's vehicle on the journey to achieving success.

A clear style of play acts as the glue that binds individuals – both players and staff – together. It is the vision that connects everyone.

A clear style of play is the *what, how, where, when* and *why*.

A clear style of play allows players to understand the ideas of the coach. It provides direction, creates cohesion and, as a result, breeds confidence. It allows players to work towards a collective goal and creates accountability through individual contribution.

What is a Style of Play?

A style of play, or playing philosophy, is basically an idea of *the way* you want to play. It's the *type* of football you *believe* in as a coach and a *blueprint* for what will bring you success.

Style of play example

"We believe in playing out from the back, managing the ball through the thirds, and being quick, clever and creative in the final third."

The above example is a basic framework that a professional football academy formed when thinking about the type of players they were seeking to create. From this coaching philosophy, they produced a style of play that included specific job descriptions for the defenders, midfielders, and attackers. Consequently, the coaching sessions were devised to develop and enhance these roles and responsibilities. The entire coaching programme was formed and continued to evolve through simply defining the way they wanted to play.

A style of play should also attempt to define the physical and psychological traits required for the players to be successful. For example, playing fast and aggressive or composed and patient adds a layer of detail and builds a clearer picture of the type of football you want to create at your club. A style of play is the blueprint that creates a team's playing identity – knowing who and what we are.

Specific Actions

Get clear about the way you want your team to play. What is the type of football you would like to play? Use the template below to assist you.

Style of Play – Six Key Questions
1. What? (What is our style of play?)
2. Why? (Why do we believe in it?)
3. Who? (Who is required to achieve it?)
4. How? (How are we going to work on it?)
5. When? (When are we going to work on it?)
6. Where? (Where can we work on it?)

Communication in Coaching

It's not what we say but the way we say it…

As coaches, we send out messages all the time, whether we are aware of it or not. Communication is constant, so we need to make it clear. The quality of our communication is defined by the quality of the response we get. As the famous saying explains, *"We cannot not communicate."*

Research suggests that 60% of all communication is non-verbal. This means that nearly two-thirds of the way we communicate is not through words but body language, facial expressions, and eye contact. A further 30% is speed, tonality, and rhythm of speech. This means that 90% of what we say, as coaches, is conveyed through *the way* that we deliver the message rather than merely what we say.

Players who are encouraged to contribute with their thoughts and ideas to share perspectives, end up collaborating and solving problems collectively. Nearly always, this process takes a little more time, but the added value of a player-led, coach-supported environment is that players own 90% of the *process*. Once the framework for your style of play is clarified, players can and will (given the opportunity through the right environment) own and commit to its delivery.

A certain amount of disagreement, providing it's always shared with the aim of being constructive, can be hugely beneficial. It's this family culture which provides the platform for players to grow and develop the true potential of resilience. Not in a soft, protected environment where everything is done for them, but one that places principles such as communication, ownership, and responsibility at the heart of its vision.

A coach needs to be highly secure within themselves in order to adopt this approach. Traditionally, the coach is king in a football club. They are the one who tells players what to do, where and how to do it, when to do it, and why. They spend countless hours leading team meetings in front of the squad, directing the game plan or dissecting previous performances. That approach is not one that the modern day emotionally-intelligent evolved coach adopts though. In fact, it's the opposite. This coach very consciously and deliberately seeks new ways to lead *through* the players; creating new and innovative ways for them to own their environment.

Sir Clive Woodward

The art of collaborative coaching methods isn't a new one. Sir Clive Woodward once told me, "There is no such thing as a dumb idea. Competitive advantage is gained only when a coach realises they don't have all the answers. The ability to be influenced and improved by their players' ideas and perceptions... this is the future leader coach." After giving a talk one day, I jumped at the opportunity to ask him a few questions. Sir Clive shared some personal experiences about his time as Head Coach of the World Cup-winning England Rugby Team.

As part of his team meetings with the players, he would ask them questions such as "What would the winning move against Australia look like?" or "Why do you think it's important that we think about dealing with pressure?" He told me his reasoning behind this approach was simply to delve into the deep veins of experience that each player brought with them from their respective clubs. With over 20 players from super elite rugby clubs, Sir Clive created the opportunity for the players and staff to share their learning process. When I asked him if the players ever taught the staff a thing or two, he smiled and said: "categorically yes." It seemed that there were times when players would reach new heights and create evolved ideas for training, practice drills, and competition.

This is my idea of a highly functioning self-sufficient organism that has the capacity to live and breathe solutions into life. This is a team environment where athletes create new levels of trust through sharing and collaboration. It's the birthplace of highly functioning independent learners. It's an environment which is conducive to freedom of expression without fear of constant judgement. And in the absence of the fear of personal judgement, authenticity flourishes. This style of coaching management appeals to the significance and experience of the players; it values their unique personal perceptions and ideas – always trusting in their judgements.

Levels of self-worth multiply through the connection formed out of positive intention for each teammate. It's an environment that enforces an underlying value that the whole is greater than one part.

Discovery learning is the opposite of giving athletes solutions to remember; it's about giving them challenges to solve. As Aristotle once put it, "He who cannot be a good follower cannot be a good leader."

What Sir Clive Woodward was actually demonstrating to his players was his capacity to relinquish his own *ego*. He acknowledged the fact that the players were closer to the solution at times than he was; after all, it was they who were actually 'in the arena' so to speak, facing the challenges head-on.

Let's look at a command coach style compared to a discovery one.

EXPLAIN YOUR STYLE OF PLAY

Fixed Command	Growth Discovery
"Listen to what I'm about to tell you."	"Let me listen to what you've got to say."
"You should feel."	"How do you feel?"
"This is the problem and this is the solution."	"How are we being challenged, and what are we learning?"
"I'll tell you what I think."	"What do you think?"
"Let me tell you what you need to do."	"Can you tell me what you need to do?"
"I want you to…"	"You decide."

It takes as much skill to ask the right type of questions, in the right way at the right time, as it does to know all the answers. What's more, the process of searching for the answers is as valuable (and sometimes more valuable) than actually getting the answer correct. But in order to create this environment, certain things are required from you as the coach.

Specific actions

- Be willing to provide your players with the means to take risks, to have a voice and ask judgement-free questions. They must know it's safe to be vulnerable to create psychological safety.
- Open up, share, and be willing to be judged by your own players. Seek their feedback about the training session or team meeting.
- Be willing to take risks, and admit when you make a mistake in front of your players.
- Admit that you don't have all the answers like Sir Clive Woodward!
- Be willing to share something personal with your players, so they know it's okay to be open.
- Vary the method of your communication style and location. Use team meetings, individual one-to-ones, and video feedback to convey your ideas and allow players to contribute.
- Keep it fun by being innovative and vary how and when you communicate. Asking other coaches to convey their ideas, and allowing players to hear a different voice, can increase variety.
- Always end on a positive in the team meeting, re-focusing the session with three main points, so everyone leaves the room clear.

PRINCIPLE 7

Ask the 'Right' Questions

> **I asked him if he understood and he said yes.
> So, he can't be confused.**
>
> Professional Coach

'Do you understand?' is a fundamentally flawed question in coaching.

Does it make logical sense? Yes.

Is it the right type of question? No.

Why? It fails to allow a player to respond in detail; to express personal levels of conceptualised understanding. It's a closed question. Understand *'what'* exactly? And *'when'* did *'it'* happen?

When you use open-ended questions with players, and when we listen to our players, we simultaneously tune into their perceptions, and get an insight into how they think, feel, and see the game. 'Why was that run important?', 'How does this pass, in this position, help us?'

- Create opportunities for players to articulate, share, and reinforce perceptual understanding.
- Use open questions to explore player learning.
- Practice listening without interrupting.
- Allow players to ask questions around specific themes.

Saying nothing is sometimes best

Saying nothing is sometimes best, but *why?*

Coaches should provide the platform for what is known in psychology as *Self-Regulation*. Ultimately, the main aim is for players to become self-sufficient so they can independently solve problems in games and in practice. As coaches, we encourage progress with constant support, and through the creation of healthy learning environments.

Often, the best way to observe whether learning has taken place is to provide the players with a platform to showcase their knowledge. How can we ever see if our players have learned, if they have never been given the opportunity to demonstrate their levels of understanding, independently, in the *absence* of constant information from the touchline? When you create a shared learning environment as a coach, you are inviting the players to co-create. Discovery learning both empowers the players and reinforces your ideas at a deeper relational level. By allowing the players a voice, and responding with respect, you develop trust.

Bite-sized is best

Our attention spans, and our ability to concentrate at length, develop over time. Adults can pay attention and concentrate for longer periods than children. Whether you're working with children or adult players, structure your message with clear, concise, simple information. Recognise players' tolerance levels for information from their responses. Coaches can over-analyse performances and provide too much information which causes hesitancy and indecision in players.

It's not about how much we know, but how much players can 'take in' when listening.

Structure practice sessions in short bursts of intense periods, matching the demands and duration of the game. Summarise main points in simple ways to make learning engaging and enjoyable!

Everyone's different

Psychometric testing (methods for testing mental capabilities and behavioural styles) is so well corroborated that it's undeniable we all have unique ways of seeing, learning about, and understanding the world around us.

Everyone's different.

But what does this really mean for coaches? It means that our players have various ways of taking in, absorbing, and interpreting the information we give them. A coach needs to cover the bases by showing, telling, and involving them in a variety of ways in training. Video clips, tactics boards, and movement pattern drills create a multi-dimensional learning environment which supports the many different learning needs.

Communicate to alleviate

When we increase the level of positive communication, we decrease anxiety. If players aren't sure about instructions, it can create anxiety. They may feel threatened and confused by uncertainty. Provide concrete examples of progress by highlighting lessons that have been learned, and clarify roles and responsibilities.

Calmly communicate areas of improvement in as many different ways as possible, creating high energy environments for learning to be varied and inspirational. Use individual and group meetings to get to know the person behind the player; progress in performance will follow.

PRINCIPLE 7

Specific actions

As we have previously covered, in Principle 5, a player's confidence is often a reflection of the coach's capacity to communicate with absolute clarity. This is important both on and off the field. You must take direct responsibility for ensuring that your players understand exactly how you want the team to play.

Gather video from training sessions and let the players feedback to each other in a unit meeting.

Make sure you, as the coach, lead a team meeting to reinforce what you want.

- Highlight three key principles and design some posters to put up in the dressing room reminding the players of what you're working towards.

- Give the team a playbook and each player a specific role/purpose with clarity about what is required from them.

- If you have one, get an analyst to film player clips of what they need to do. Use training examples or role models from the very highest level of the game. If you don't have an analyst – ask a friend to video your games, or build your own library of clips from YouTube. Start with what you have.

- If you get a chance, build a bank of videos for each position; get your players to watch clips for each unit (goalkeepers, defenders, midfielders, attackers) and ask them to come back and report on the top three roles and responsibilities for their teammates.

- Show players the training schedule that highlights each day's practice theme/aspect of play. Which days will be double/treble sessions? When will they get the opportunity to do extra practice in units?

- Set a meeting to discuss how sports science, and strength and conditioning coaches (if you have them), will integrate. What will the warm-up look like? Warm up with the ball, position-specific warm up, ball work, possession, team play, tactical session and game phase? Adjust the depth and detail of information you give to the level, age, and ability of your players; most importantly, use this detail to inspire and energise players to learn more about themselves and the improvements they can make.

Summary

Establishing a clear style of play is a sure fire way to create a competitive advantage. A clear style of play binds both players and staff to a shared mental model that cements understanding and boosts confidence.

As coaches, establishing a playing identity on the field through purposeful practice is fundamental. When you reinforce this identity through working on your style of play off the field, you enhance your capacity to create your team's confidence through clarity. Doing this in an environment that is co-created empowers players to own their style of play through shared collaboration; in doing so, you will create fully functioning independent learners.

PRINCIPLE 8
80:20

Most coaches revert back to nullifying their opponents' strengths by (primarily) planning to *stop* the other team. This is, it would seem, a perfectly rational first port of call. But, all too often, in an attempt to fully inform players of their opponents' strengths, coaches overcompensate and focus completely on the opposition's skillset at the expense of neglecting their own team's abilities.

There is a very important difference between two particular mindsets that coaches must understand when preparing a team to perform. To illustrate the difference, let's play a quick game. Just follow the instructions.

1. Don't think about a pink elephant. Do not think about a big pink elephant with big ears. Do not see a vision of a pink elephant.
2. Thought of a pink elephant yet?

In Neuro-Linguistic Programming (NLP) this is what's known as a *negative command*. Using negative commands is one way of sending subliminal messages to the brain. The unconscious mind cannot process the negative, only the positive messages register (*Think about a pink elephant*). That's why, for around 95% of people who play this game, people always see a pink elephant.

In this simple game, it doesn't really matter if you see a pink elephant or not, but what if we were to put this into a different context? Imagine a coach who is preparing his or her team to play. Imagine they are focusing on their opponents' strengths during their team talk and emphasising them with a negative command: "Don't get too close to the striker when you mark them at the corner or he will score." What message would the player receive? The players' unconscious minds would receive the instruction to *get close to the striker and mark them at the corner.*

With the best of intentions, and in an attempt to help their players combat the opposition's strengths, the coach has actually ended up instructing the players' unconscious mind to do the very thing they didn't want them to do!

This simple act of mis-programming takes place all the time in dressing rooms up and down the country at all levels. And the solution is obvious and simple. As the coach, instead of telling the players what you *don't want* them to do, tell them what you *do want* them to do. In the above example, it would simply be: "Leave some space when marking the striker at the corner and you will win the ball."

The second pitfall when preparing your team to play is focusing too much on the opposition's skill-set, potential threat, and ability. A team that focuses only on their opponents (and how dangerous they are) falls prey to exaggerating their perceived power and the opposing team gets lifted onto a self-created pedestal of superiority. Your team will become exhausted and starved of thinking about their own strengths. Instead of succumbing to this common pitfall, feed your players with the solutions that combat each strength of the opposition. Focus 20% of your attention on the opposition's strengths and 80% on how your team is going to beat them. This will build confidence and paint pictures of how to unhinge the opposition's weaknesses.

No Limit Thinking

> **A pessimist sees the difficulty in every opportunity;**
> **an optimist sees the opportunity in every difficulty.**
>
> Winston Churchill

Many of the limits we experience in our performances, and our lives, are self-created thanks to faulty thinking processes. A mind full of doubt and fear will inevitably limit success and lead to failure. By taking control of our thoughts, we can remove these self-imposed barriers. A mind full of belief, hope, and optimism generates successful '*being*' and successful '*doing*' from which come positive results.

> **Whether you think you can, or you think you can't, you're right.**
>
> Henry Ford

Jack Butland's No Limit Thinking

2012 saw the European Championships co-hosted by Poland and Ukraine. The then England manager, Roy Hodgson, called up the youngest goalkeeper the country had seen for over 100 years: Birmingham City's Jack Butland. Jack was only 19-years-old when he made his international debut. You could forgive a player for being boastful about such a historical call-up. To think he was special or that he had 'made it' even.

But when I asked Jack how he felt about his role in the most important soccer tournament of his life, his response was surprisingly modest: "Happy and humble, Tom, you know me."

Everything Jack stood for was being recognised at the highest level, something he had worked tirelessly for every single day of his life. Yet he was meeting this opportunity with total humility for the occasion and absolute confidence in himself.

Humility + Supreme Confidence = Success.

Jack was setting records and making headlines as England's youngest ever goalkeeper, but he had already honed the mindset of a seasoned champion. A mindset that welcomed limitless thinking.

The Why Not Voice Within

Jack and I would often talk about what great possibilities lay ahead and the excitement of the inevitable opportunities that would arise in the future. When they would come, we didn't know. One thing was for sure, though, we were not anticipating events to come as early as Euro 2012.

But Jack was ready because Jack always asked himself 'Why Not?' We called this his 'Why Not Voice' from within. It's a state of constant readiness, of no limit thinking. Dreams become realities with constant action, so Jack's 'Why Not Voice' saw the inevitability of this opportunity. But it wasn't an arrogance he displayed. It was humility.

Supreme Confidence

That's the second thing about elite performers. They don't confuse an inner conviction with superficial arrogance. Confidence comes from the courage to face areas for improvement with an action-orientated Response-ABLE mindset. This process results in high levels of self-worth and inner conviction.

Carlos Castaneda captured the essence of self-worth beautifully when he wrote: "Most of our energy goes into upholding our own self-importance. If we were capable of losing some of that importance, two extraordinary things would happen to us. One we would free our energy from trying to maintain the illusory idea of our grandeur and two, we would provide ourselves with enough energy to catch a glimpse of the actual grandeur of the universe."

As Fiona Harrold puts it quite brilliantly in her empowering book, *Be Your Own Life Coach*, real power comes from self-reliance and those who have this internal power stand out from others. Self-reliance is born from a solid inner conviction, a kind of absolute knowing and independence from others. Self-reliance is a form of self-trust, a power that exists deep within a person.

Jack possessed this self-reliance, this inner conviction, and he constantly demonstrated it. One of Jack's Birmingham City teammate's observed: "Everything he does has an authority about it. He's too good for this level. The way he holds himself, the way he stands and even just puts on his boots. He's a Premier League player for sure."

Honing Jack's No Limit Thinking

Jack's career path was not always positive. Following a loan spell at Cheltenham, he found himself back at Birmingham City FC. Although Jack was back up the leagues, he was being overlooked for the first team. He was feeling the frustration of non-selection, and thought patterns of a limited mindset were at risk of developing; so I set him a challenge. The first part of the challenge was to identify lessons available from his experience. This is what he had learned:

1. Have patience.
2. Stay positive and work harder.
3. Write down career goals.
4. Have a plan but be flexible.

With these lessons in mind, Jack and I worked at length to make them part of his repertoire. We explored the principle of improving confidence and positivity through asserting powerful body language. We developed different ways to re-focus and think calmly under pressure. We would run through each game scenario and play these vividly and clearly in the mind's eye, a form of visualisation. I would ask him: "What can you see? What is the pitch like? How did you claim the ball from the inswinging corner? Where does the ball land when you kick out of your hands to start the counter?" This was part of Jack's complete preparation plan, personally designed to transfer him into his zone of focus.

An athlete's willingness to play ideas through, and tailor their own pre-performance habits, is a key sign of a champion's mindset. Jack was a young man with an insatiable thirst for competing every day in order to improve constantly. He did, and does, have a deep driving desire to learn and get better. These traits he acquired and enhanced from a young age and they continue to fuel his developing career.

Committed to these lessons, Over the next six months, Jack went on to play for Great Britain at the 2012 London Olympic games and was called up to the England senior national squad. As this shift and career acceleration began, Jack believed (and still believes) there are no limits to what he can achieve. He is a fantastic example of what can be achieved with a dream that starts with *no limit thinking*.

Champion Coaches and Players are No Limit Thinkers

Champion coaches and players create limitless mindsets and construct inspired outcomes in their lives by:

- Having Great Intentions.
- Taking Massive Action.
- Removing Doubt Totally.

For great players, coaches, and teams to perform at their peak, they must:

- Remove self-identified limiting thoughts.
- Accept that anything is possible with sufficient focus and effort.
- Understand that the strength of the effort will be the measure of the result.

I can is 100 times more powerful than IQ.

Max Lucado

Limited Thinking = Limited Performance

PRINCIPLE 8

Performing to Expectations

Perhaps not surprisingly, when we study the greats, they openly reveal again and again that they *believed* they could be great before they actually *became* great. There's not one champion who said to themselves before competition, "I'm not good enough to be here." Herein lies an interesting concept. Expectations are extremely powerful; they act as a set of mental instructions our minds subsequently carry out. Our expectations are the filter through which we see ourselves and what can be achieved in the world around us.

As human beings, we teach ourselves consciously (and most of the time sub-consciously) to live out these expectations – be they positive or negative. In sport, as in life, these expectations become the blueprint from which players deny their achievement potential. Whether you know it, or not, everything you currently see and experience in your life is a direct response to what you *believe* and expect for yourself. You have created the life and performance level you're currently at, as a direct result of the beliefs and expectations you have for yourself. And it is the same for your players. Players rarely exceed the self-image they create for themselves. A player who believes they belong on the international stage has a far greater chance of realising this dream than a player who doesn't share this belief. Players who really want to achieve something will work hard on what they *believe* is possible for themselves.

Terry Cole-Whittaker offered one of the best book titles for keeping out the dream stealers. In her book entitled *What You Think of Me is None of My Business*, she fixes upon the cornerstone of the no limit thinker: self-worth. Champions thrive on high self-worth, realising that '*I have to believe in me*' before others will. Some players have an inherent sense of self-worth that can be noticed through their commitment, focus, and resolve.

"Around 90 % of you in the room today, listening to me right here and now, will not make it as a professional footballer at this football club."

That was my opening line at the very first squad psychology session I hosted with the U18s at AFC Bournemouth in the summer of 2005. I will never forget that session.

Looking back at it now, as I write these words, I can still see the picture of Sam's face, as he sat there in the front row and his eyes caught mine. There was a steely look of defiance written across his face, coupled with an unmistakable glare of determination. He seemed wholly undistracted by the classroom mutters. It was the look a champion gives when they lose a point, take a hit, or miss a shot.

There was something different about Sam compared to the rest of the squad when I opened the session with that line, and I noticed it immediately. If coaches observe players carefully enough, subtle reactions to statements like these can distinguish fighters from victims, winners from losers, and leaders from followers. I could see it in the room immediately. Some players looked away and avoided eye contact, others shrugged their shoulders, others slumped in their chairs and looked at the head coach for some kind of validation of how to think or feel. Sam was none of these things. From that day, I knew he would succeed. "Who was the boy sat in the centre of the front row?" I asked the head coach. "Sam Vokes," he replied with a smile of recognition, and approval that I had picked a player he held high hopes for.

Anything is POSSIBLE when players *truly* BELIEVE in themselves

The entire second youth team session I delivered that day was based on one simple principle: self-belief. And the term "self-belief" sat on the presentation board in front of the players for the full hour. Deliberately, it was the only slide. The purpose? To train the sub-conscious mind through positive emotional reinforcement. During the session, I asked the players to note down, on a sheet of paper, what this statement meant to them and how it made them feel.

Some of the boys would have thrown the sheet away, I'm sure, whilst others would have put it in their folders for it to become 'another piece of paper', but for Sam, it went straight up on his bedroom wall. That's the key to affirmations. They're not just meaningless statements. When they're used properly, they can invoke powerful emotional changes that embed positive thinking and feeling. Sam used this affirmation to its maximum. He would think about what it really meant to him. He would imagine how it felt to be in the image he created for himself. He was wiring his neurology for success, training his brain, attracting successful opportunities.

For a player, there's no better feeling than envisaging a scenario on the pitch play out in their mind's eye, prior to the game in real time. When this happens, they've already seen events unfold, and they already know how it feels. They know exactly what to do when the ball falls a certain way, because they have already done it in a visualisation. They are prepared for their moments of opportunity, both emotionally and neurologically.

This mental and emotional preparation was part of Sam's routine. He took it seriously, focused intently, and made it part of his training programme. Once again, he was demonstrating that to obtain better results he had to be open-minded enough to think differently. Most players, most people, want new and different results but they stay stuck in the same habits that form their routine. Einstein once said that repeatedly doing the same things and expecting different results is the definition of insanity. Sam, however, worked with an open mind, honest heart, and determined spirit. These things became the foundation of our work together, a crucial ingredient that helped him with his transition into the professional game.

It wasn't until I saw Sam, a couple of years later, after his move to Wolverhampton Wanderers FC that he told me he had kept his affirmation sheet and put it up on the wall in his new house. He still uses it to this day. The very same piece of paper – in a glass frame – it reads "Anything is possible when I truly believe in myself."

Muhammad Ali's Self-Belief: Power of the Inner Voice

In 1964, at 22 years of age, Cassius Marcellus Clay, Jr, stepped into the ring against Sonny Liston to challenge for the world heavyweight title. Before the fight, such was the expectation that Liston would beat Clay, the stadium was only half full. Liston had it all: the strength, the size, the reach, and the experience.

But the legend that would be Muhammad Ali had a greater strength: brains over brawn. He studied everything about Liston before the fight. "I read everything I could where he had been interviewed. I talked with people who had been around him or who had talked with him. I would lie in bed at night and put all of these things together thinking about them and would try to get a picture of how his mind worked." Before the fight, Ali told the world he was 'the greatest', later revealing in an autobiography that he had to keep saying it until he made himself believe it. At a time when most fighters let their managers do the talking, Ali would speak up. He was articulate, bold, and funny. He easily controlled press conferences and interviews, spoke freely and intelligently about issues unrelated to boxing, and offered rhymes that humorously denigrated his opponents (even predicting the round in which "they must fall").

Cassius Clay won the fight and the rest, of course, is history.

Here's what the great Muhammad Ali taught the world:

- Accept no limitations.
- Believe in yourself even if, and especially if, others around you don't.
- Don't let the noise of other people's opinions drown out your own inner voice.
- Be brave enough to be different to achieve extraordinary results.
- Those people who are crazy enough to believe they can change the world are usually the ones that do.
- Be prepared to pay the price for the success and achievement you strive for.

We Create the Good Days and the Bad

The truth is that we are the sole creators of our own realities according to our beliefs and expectations. We should all examine these carefully. If we do not like some aspect of our world, it is worth examining our own expectations. It takes practice to realise that experiences are often no more than a materialisation of our beliefs.

If you find positivity, health, happiness, and smiles on the faces of those you meet, then realise that your beliefs are beneficial.

If you see a world that is good, a world of joy, again take it that your beliefs are healthy. But, if you find negativity, ill health, a lack of meaningful work, and a world of sorrow, then it's time to re-examine your beliefs and begin to change them at once.

You must learn to erase a negative thought or picture by replacing it with its opposite.

Jane Roberts

The same goes for your players.

This does not mean to say that we want players to create a world of positive illusion pretending not to see difficulties that arise. But it means helping them to choose to focus on making things better by finding solutions through the way they think. It's not pretending there aren't any challenges in life; it's paying attention to the abundance of inner resources and finding the opportunity to overcome challenges.

Take criticism as an example. In elite sport, it's par for the course. We know if players want to improve and work towards fulfilling their potential, they need to be able to take criticism on board and use it to propel their game forwards. All too often, players react defensively to well-meaning criticism, or take less than complimentary opinions to heart. Players who can only hear the negative, and find it hard to use criticism positively, set limits on their game. These players think "I can't" rather than "I can" and sometimes wonder if what they were trying to do during a game was *impossible*.

Instead of setting up mental roadblocks to success, I like to tell my athletes to respond in a certain way to this limited impossible thinking. When we study the word impossible and break it into two, we literally get *'I'm Possible'*. Impossible is just an opinion, and the champion athletes refuse to let the noise associated with other people's opinions or their negative selves drown out their own inner voices of self-belief. It's the coaches who encourage their athletes to dare to be magnificent, who help develop the superstars of the international stage. As the great Sir Winston Churchill said, ignore the critics, "you'll never reach your destination if you stop and throw stones at every dog that barks." I'm certain that *no limit thinkers* would rather choke on greatness than nibble on mediocrity.

Our experience of the world is formed as a faithful replica of our own thoughts, and thoughts possess energy. Positive thoughts provide ammunition to empower the mind. As a coach, you are in a position to help players erase any negative limited thinking by replacing it with a positive alternative. When players learn to do this well, they form a reality that will help them develop a no limit mindset that focuses on what is possible.

The Science behind Visualisation

> **If you can see it in your mind, you're going to hold it in your hand.**
> The Secret

For the first time, scientists can prove that when visualising actions, at least two-thirds of the brain's activity activates in a similar way to actual physical practice. Based on modern day advances in technology and the advent of neuroscience, it is now indisputable that the same areas of the brain – the same neural pathways, and the same synaptic events –

activate when a player is visualising effectively, as when they physically practice for real.

When an athlete visualises a movement, the message originates in an area of the brain called the primary motor cortex, then travels via the lower brain into the secondary motor cortex, eventually ending up in the prefrontal cortex where a mental image is then formed.

We now know that exactly the same process takes place in the brain when an athlete performs physically. But instead of the message being fired into the prefrontal cortex (as with visualisation), it is transported to the central nervous system to make muscles move. So, for reinforcing mental instructions and representations, visualisation is as good as physical practice, with some additional advantages. For example, when a player performs for real, they don't have the opportunity to 'rewind and re-focus' on the outcomes. During visualisation, they can replay moves, access their full spectrum of emotions, and retune undesired outcomes. That's why it is so important that the visualisation is real.

If an athlete is frustrated in their performance, I ask them to be frustrated in their image, and overcome that frustration. If they are upset in their performance situation, I ask them to be upset in their image, and conquer it. If they are nervous in their performance environment, I ask them to be nervous in their image and transcend it. This way, visualisation provides a solid, real experience that the athletes can relate to, feel, and lock into their performance mindset. In other words, having seen themselves in their mind overcome the challenge, the emotional brain positively rewires itself, attuning an individual's focus toward success, energy, and achievement. Once they've overcome the challenge they face in their image, it's important that a player focuses and enjoys how good it feels to be in the successful part of the mental picture they've formed. When this is done on a regular basis, and combined with physical practice out on the training field, the results can be immediate and astonishing.

Elite performers remain separate from the outcome, immersed in the process, and detached from the good opinion of other people. In this place, total self-reliance and inner security is born. It's what Abraham Maslow tried to define in his descriptions of the 'self-actualised' being. One who lives a life of meaning and purpose, totally connected to a high self-worth, and liberated through the freedom of inner security. They see solutions where others see problems and choice in the challenges they face to overcome them. No limit thinkers are undeterred by the naysayers and driven by a "why not" voice within. A no limit thinker becomes even more determined if presented with 'proof' that something can't be done.

Advances in cognitive research now show that a thought a) possesses energy and b) can be measured. Using a machine called an Electroencephalograph (EEG), the frequency of thoughts can be observed and pinpointed, to determine the speed and force of each one, just like physical muscles in the body can be.

The nature and energy of a positive thought can be life-changing. Never before in the history of modern science have we been able to confirm what we have long believed. Thoughts possess energy and thinking happy thoughts literally has the power to change and improve your physical and hormonal state.

The way we see and perceive the world, whether accurate or not becomes our reality.

Wayne Dyer

But the really fascinating thing about this notion is that the thought, or belief, doesn't even have to hold any real justifiable 'truth' to the outside world; just so long as the believer buys in.

Recently, a physiotherapist was relaying an experience to me about an ultrasound treatment he was giving to a player with a muscle strain. The player hopped up onto the bed, ready and waiting to receive his treatment, following which the physiotherapist applied the gel, worked his way around the injured area, and proceeded with the therapy. When he had finished, after around 10 minutes, the physiotherapist asked the player how he felt. "So much better," the player replied thanking the physiotherapist for his time and effort. What the player didn't know, as he walked out of the room, was that the physiotherapist had forgotten to plug the machine in.

Your Beliefs Become Your Thoughts.

Your Thoughts Become Your Words.

Your Words Become Your Actions.

Your Actions Become Your Habits.

Your Habits Become Your Values.

Your Values Become Your Destiny.

Mahatma Gandhi

The Biology of Self-Belief

The 'placebo effect' is a fascinating concept, whereby benefits are felt solely because an individual believes they will be experienced. To illustrate, let's look at an example from the field of medicine. A surgeon in America offered ten patients the opportunity to have an operation to relieve arthritic pain in their knees. Out of the ten patients, only five were given the authentic operation. The remaining five were given a small incision to replicate the marks of surgery.

Six months later, the patients were called back into the hospital to report how their knees were feeling. All ten reported that their arthritic pain was much better. For the five patients who didn't have the operation, yet *believed* that they did, physical pain had ceased to exist. One member of the placebo group, Tim Perez, went from walking with a cane to now playing basketball with his grandchildren post fake surgery. When he found out, two years later, that the surgery was in fact not real, he reflected: "In this world, anything is possible when you put your mind to it. I know that your mind can work miracles."

The strength and conviction of a personal belief has the potential to shape an entire lifetime, be it positive or negative. It matters not how bizarre the belief is, only that we wholeheartedly accept it as our personal truth. When we truly recognise that our beliefs are that powerful, we hold the key to freedom. Positive thoughts are a biological mandate for a happy, healthy life.

No Limits Thinking Comes With Doing What Makes You Happy

In his spectacularly insightful book, *The Happiness Advantage*, Shawn Achor reveals that for decades, generations have been told that if we work hard, we will be successful, and only when we are successful can we be happy. He illustrates that this famously flawed ideology has been replaced, and the most successful leading organisations, competing at the highest level, practice a different approach. Instead, choose to be, do *what makes us happy*, and we will attain an elevated mood state causing us to feel more motivated which, in turn, drives us to be more successful. Happiness is the centre of the personal universe we create for ourselves and the success we attract revolves around it.

Henry David Thoreau most eloquently conveyed this concept when he said: "When one advances confidently in the direction of his own dreams and endeavours, to live the life which he has imagined, he will come to meet with a success unexpected in common hours."

It is likely that every one of your players began playing for the joy and happiness the sport brought to them. Over the years, this enjoyment can be forgotten and the reason for playing morphs from "because it makes me happy" to "because I want to be the best" or "I want to win the league." A player's focus changes from putting happiness first, to putting success first.

There's nothing wrong with wanting to win, but if it is all a player desires, then they are more likely to play a limited game. These players will be scared of losing and won't take risks. These players will react negatively to matches lost and fail to negotiate setbacks. Sometimes players need to be reminded of the original (and real) reason they play. Playing for the love of the game will help free up a mind towards no limit thinking.

When we boldly pursue our deepest and most meaningful desires, connected by virtue of positive intention for ourselves and others, success becomes inevitable. That's the magic and power of living a no limit life.

When we remove the perceived limits that we attach to our lives, we simultaneously open up a whole new flow of personal potential. We encounter a deeper realisation. That the only limits that exist in our lives are the ones we place on ourselves and therefore are in control to remove.

The Power of Optimism - Opportunities not Limits

> **Where our thoughts go, energy flows.**
> The Secret

Great Britain and England female senior international footballer Karen Carney played against the boys in the playground who were faster, bigger, and more technical. The girls' team didn't exist back then, so when faced with the option of choosing a different sport or following her passion, there was only going to be one outcome. Over time, Karen improved rapidly due to her surroundings, not just competing but beating the boys at their own game. She did so well that she was eventually selected for the school team, not the girls' team but the boys! Karen didn't see limits; she saw opportunity. She has gone on to have a truly fantastic career as one of England's most cherished female footballers.

Helping Players Train the Brain

So, having seen the power of positive thinking, optimism, and belief – the real question is, can we train brains to be more positive? Can minds be taught to simply think happier and more constructive thoughts? Well, here's where it gets fascinating. Neuroscientists suggest that we have between 90,000 and 120,000 thoughts per day, most of which are recurring, and that we are unaware of. This means that we have an astounding number of recurring *sub-conscious* thoughts that are responsible for the emotional states we experience and which we create for ourselves. In other words, the very blueprint for the way we feel is constructed via autopilot!

But what if you were able to interrupt this habitual way of thinking and feed yourself healthier, more empowered thoughts in order to supercharge beliefs and heighten expectations? What if the way our brains operate could be changed to live a more inspired, limitless life… a life of unlimited potential?

The work of Dr. Bruce Lipton suggests we can. His work into epigenetics suggests that positive, healthy, inspired thinkers are not only changing their brains but they are transforming their entire being, improving the very construction of their genetics. After years of scientific exploration as a cell biologist, Dr. Lipton has dedicated an entire lifetime of research toward understanding the biochemical effects of the brain's functioning. His stunning discoveries indicate unequivocally that our thoughts influence precise molecular pathways and their functioning. In other words, our thoughts, largely determined by our perceptions, create not just our mental but physical reality too, at a real and tangible molecular level. He wrote: "I suddenly realised that a cell's life is fundamentally controlled by the physical and energetic environment with only a small contribution by its genes. The character of our lives is determined not by our genes but by our responses that propel life."

In essence, it's not the conditions we face but the decisions we make that determine the shape of our lives. We can't always control the situations and circumstances we face, but we can always control our responses to those conditions. At a very real physical, emotional, and mental level, this knowledge can empower us to make positive, lasting changes.

There are hormonal improvements too. Research from adolescent soccer players shows that when coaches focus on encouraging the performances of their teams during half-time talks (as opposed to berating them) hormonal increases in testosterone, serotonin, and dopamine (positive hormones) rise to aid performance. These hormones assist muscular contraction, and support the brain in its attempts to retain emotional balance. These hormones are crucial in making movements quicker and more powerful, and preventing the onset of cardiovascular, mental, and emotional fatigue. These hormones are critical to performance for both body and mind. In comparison, players who are subjected to intense criticism in a disempowering environment have lower levels of all three empowering, immune-boosting hormones.

Knowing the benefits of thinking positively for his game, one young international developed a pre-match routine he followed the night before every game. This routine involved thinking in a very deliberate way that reinforced focus, confidence, and resolve for the upcoming contest.

- He reminds himself what he has done well in preparation for the game:

  "I know I have done everything I can to be ready for the game when I was at home and during pre-season."

  "I know all of my equipment is ready for tomorrow."

- He reinforces how he wants, and deserves, to be feeling:

  "I am relaxed and excited."

  "I'm feeling good, very excited for the start of the game tomorrow."

- He reaffirms his sense of robust self-confidence:

  "I know I am ready for any challenges I am faced with tomorrow."

  "I am ready to go."

By doing the above before every match, the player created a performance focus and heightened his sense of self-determination. By refusing to let his inner flame go out, he produced excellent performances for his club and country. He took control of the things he was in control of, and let go of the things he couldn't.

So what can we do, practically, to help players think positively and reap all these benefits? Below are a set of exercises you can use with your players to help free their minds from having limited thought patterns, to honing no limit thinking.

Specific actions

As an 80:20 coach, you consciously structure team meetings and player interactions to focus on players' own internal skills and strengths. This is not the same as saying 'let's pretend the opposition don't have any strengths'. It means that you do not overemphasise these strengths and prevent your players from feeling anxious. Instead, you create a healthy feeling of conviction about how to *overcome* the challenge with multiple solutions which prepare the team to win.

1. Acknowledge players' areas for improvement whilst appealing to a sense of inevitable growth and development.
2. Take the time to challenge players when they over-criticise themselves and work with them to improve each day, providing constant feedback and communication on how to progress. Interrupting the pattern of too much negative self-talk prevents players from unhelpful self-created pessimism and doubt.
3. Instead, take the time to get to know your players' hopes and dreams. Find out what they dream of achieving and why. This will get them to focus on their inspiration and at the same time allow you to support them to achieve it.
4. Share you own personal dream, career ambition, or personal achievement goal with the team.
5. Create a team vision board, detailing the team's goals and ambitions for the game, the month or the season. Put this in the dressing room or canteen for them to see every time they walk in.

Exercises

1. Take time to study the opposition and pick out their three main strengths as a team and three best players. Using film footage, photos, or a flip chart, share these strengths in simple detail with your team to make them fully aware.

Example:

1. The opponents play long balls into the air between our full backs and wingers to win second balls with force
2. This team will sit deep and deny spaces between the units and lines getting 11 men behind the ball to counter fast
3. They have three main ways to counter on the wings and in central areas (show these)

Critically, having explained the strengths and strategies of the opposition, provide clear, simple and specific instruction on how to respond whilst appealing to your team's skillset.

Example:

PRINCIPLE 8

1. To prevent them playing these high balls in between our full backs and wide-men, our front three – David, John and Danny – you are going to press high, using your pace and strength to stop them playing. When you win the ball high up the pitch, counter at speed in central areas and we will score!

2. When they sit deep we can be patient with the ball. They will tire. We can beat them through, round, or over their deep-lying defensive block like this (show the team three simple strategies).

3. To prevent the counter, we will defend whilst attacking. To do this our full backs – Gary and Alex – you will take up this position to be available to support the attack but close enough to recover when required.

*Important. When you provide ways to beat the opposition in specific situations, use personal examples: call names out, make eye contact, and take your time with one to ones. Show examples of the opposition failing on film. Provide your players with examples of why the opposition didn't succeed and how to beat them.

- Host a pre-training meeting to illustrate and highlight what the training session will be about and why it is important ahead of game day. This is your opportunity to help your players link their learning in training to game day demands.

- Provide your players with three strengths as an action plan to execute before each game. Be simple and specific. Write them up and post each plan above their peg in the dressing room. For a number 10 this could be;

Example: - *Receive and turn quickly between the lines – Shoot from distance whenever you can – Find the pocket of space between the 4 and 8 on transition from defence to attack*

As we've mentioned several times during this book, meeting with the players one to one is a great way of providing assurance and direction in a personal way. For the players, running through their objectives or clarifying the game plan the day before the game can be extremely beneficial. If you have access, provide video clips that outline your message and help the player see your ideas and instruction. Always finish on a positive.

Summary

As a coach adopting the 80:20 Principle, you are fully aware of the opposition's strengths but do not overemphasise them. You fuel your players with multiple solutions to combat their opponents and instil a heightened sense of self-belief. Through reinforcing these strengths before the game, and providing many solutions to the challenges they may face, players enter the competitive arena fully prepared and flexible enough to adapt to any situation.

80:20 coaches acknowledge the reality of the challenge but refuse to get stuck over-thinking or worrying. Instead, they plough their mental and emotional energy into the solution required and transfer their mental belief into that game plan. 80:20 coaches believe there is always a way forward. 80:20 coaches are no limit thinkers.

No limit thinkers define their potential by dreaming big dreams. They are unafraid of sharing these dreams with others, and they take action every single day to step toward their goals. They align their expectations to their high aspirations, and seek to improve constantly. Where others see limitations, struggles, and setbacks, no limit optimists find solutions. They see choice in their challenges and rise to new levels. When you live with a no limit perspective, the possibilities are endless. Champion athletes who perform with this mindset believe in themselves before anyone else does.

The energy that positive thinking brings us is now well proven in science. When you re-affirm a positive belief over and over again, and take action toward your goals on a regular basis, progress is not only possible, it's inevitable. Anyone, who has achieved anything will testify that they first had to expect it from themselves.

Limitations are nothing more than perceptions. When we remove the perceived limits that we attach to our performances and our lives, we simultaneously open up a whole new flow of personal potential. The only limits that exist are the ones we place on ourselves through our thinking. We can remove them. Anything is possible when we truly believe in ourselves.

PRINCIPLE 9
MANAGING SELF

> **The health of the team is reflected in the face of the coach.**
> Bill Beswick

Gameday provides the occasion for magical moments to occur. As coach, *your* attitude, energy, and emotion is often the driving force behind the entire team's atmosphere, mood, and environment. As coach, players and staff look to you for how to behave, think, and feel. As coach, you are the architect of the emotional climate. For this reason, managing gameday is, in reality, about managing yourself.

> **Knowing others is intelligence;**
> **Knowing yourself is true wisdom.**
> **Mastering others is strength;**
> **Mastering yourself is true power.**
> Lao Tzu - Tao Te Ching

Cool and Calm Breeds Clear and Confident

Think back to the story in Principle 2 – the 2012 match between FC Barcelona's U18 side, and Bayer Leverkusen, at the Sporting City. The German coach bounded up and down the touchline with a clipboard and whistle barking orders out to his players. Barcelona's coaches sat calmly in the shade of the dugout. The game, very evenly matched, finished 1-1 but I was fascinated by the difference in coaching behaviours and the impact they had on the players during the game. Leverkusen's players were clearly struggling to listen to the coach, find their positions, track the ball and keep focus. Barcelona's players, in the absence of their coaches' constant intervention, were able to find their own rhythm with each other.

Remember what the U18 FC Barcelona youth coach said when I asked him why he didn't intervene from the touchline? He smiled, and simply said, "If we coach the players during match day, how will we ever get to understand how much they know? Matchday is their opportunity to demonstrate their learning from the week and show, independently of us, how much they know. The result is never the most important outcome. The demonstration of learning is most important for us."

The coaches knew that coaching the team during the game that day would actively hinder their players' chances of developing thinking skills that would tackle performance challenges calmly. They were living out the principle of remaining cool and calm to breed players that will be clear and confident in their thinking. Does this mean the players made more 'mistakes'? Potentially, yes. But, that's the point. That's the power. Learning to think independently, wrestle and struggle with failure, and learn as a result. The outcome? A creative solution-orientated mindset that fosters perseverance. Allowing the players the freedom to engage with their own failings during the match, without 'quick fix' coaching techniques, is a guaranteed way to help them more in the long run.

Only a secure coach who does not fear the scoreline of defeat, and what it means about their own coaching ability, can breed this type of thinking player. Coaches must learn to coach for the players and not themselves. They must be strong enough to overcome their own insecurity of what defeat means about them and their ability to coach. They must learn to disassociate themselves from the result and base their value not on the outcome of winning the game, but on creating thinking players.

This may seem a little contradictory by nature, if you're reading and thinking about this concept for the first time, but let's just consider the alternative for a second. Let's say the Barcelona coaches intervened straightaway with tactical information to instantly correct their team's deficiencies. Would it improve their chances of winning the game? Probably, but, coaching for the 'quick win' ultimately prevents long-term learning because you remove the player's ability to think under pressure in the moment and find solutions. The ultimate measure of success for the Barcelona coaches – at this development level – is whether or not the player can learn the tactical intelligence and emotional control required to play for the first team. They place the player in the centre, and in doing so, remove their own sense of self-importance which is defined by much more than the final score.

5 Questions for Coaches on Matchday:

1. How would I describe my behaviour during the game?
2. How do I normally feel when the game is going on?
3. How would it feel to be coached by me on matchday?

4. How do I create a learning environment for my players on matchday?
5. What does 'success' mean to me on matchday?

Specific Actions

1. Emotionally lead your team under pressure by emotionally leading yourself first.
2. Define your own success which is not just based on the scoreline... what *is* winning?
3. Place your players' needs above your own and see the world through their eyes. List your players' needs, then actively create coaching strategies to respond. For example, if a player needs to feel significant, your strategy might be for the player to lead the warm up and cool down with the team (in the absence of the coach). As such, the player feels valued and significant due to being trusted to lead an important aspect of training.

Usain Bolt – Knowing Self

Usain Bolt did not fit the orthodox stereotype of a 100m gold medal-winning sprinter. World record 100m sprint times are defined by a quick, sharp, and powerful explosion out of the blocks. The start is crucial and should define the rest of the race. Usain Bolt's starts failed to fit this description.

Bolt had the size, but he ran all wrong. His starts were notoriously slow sometimes even falling behind the rest of the runners; he appeared to take longer strides at the wrong times and come up far too early. Yet, instead of trying to change his start style, Usain Bolt developed reassurance from his awareness and understanding of his strengths. He said, "For me, a good reaction is key because I'm a poor starter, but if I get a good reaction I can get myself into the race even if my first couple of steps are not quick." In the last 40m of any race, he could tell if he was going to win it or not. Why? Because the last 40m of any race was the very strongest part of his race. At a height of 6'5", he was the tallest athlete in the history of sprinting, taking 41 steps on average at a stride length of roughly 2.44m over 100 metres.

Clearly, one ingredient to Bolt's success was the genetic inheritance he was blessed with, born into a fast masterpiece of a body equipped perfectly for athletics. Yet, in other ways, he defied the sport he dominated, and did not relent when others voiced negative opinions of his unorthodox and limited running style. Here's what Usain Bolt reminds us of.

- Do not let what you can't do get in the way of what you can.
- Minimise your weaknesses by maximising your strengths.
- Love, enjoy, and celebrate what you are passionate about.

Managing My State

The following model was inspired by an Anthony Robbins seminar I attended, in Fiumicino, Italy, back in 2009. Although I've adapted the model slightly here, it encompasses the same principles. Essentially, our emotional states are transitory. In other words, they often change from positive to negative, frustrated to euphoric, or sad to happy. Most of us don't realise, however, that we have the power to change these emotional states, whenever we want, through understanding some very basic principles. Namely, you can change your emotional state through three main elements, all of which are constantly interchanging and connected. An understanding of how these principles work can change your emotional state and help define your path to achieving peak performance.

Three State-Changing Influences

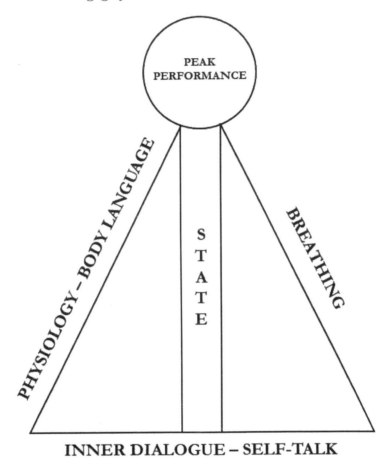

PHYSIOLOGY – BODY LANGUAGE

PEAK PERFORMANCE

S T A T E

BREATHING

INNER DIALOGUE – SELF-TALK

Let's explore these three components in a little more detail.

Inner Dialogue or Self-Talk

Each of us has an internal voice. Whether we like to admit it or not (and whether we are aware of it or not) we also 'talk' to ourselves with that internal voice. Sometimes out loud, sometimes in our heads as thoughts. And no, it doesn't make you crazy! Here are three things you need to know about your internal voice.

1. It likes to talk.
2. It can be positive or negative.
3. It repeats itself.

Take a look at what England Goalkeeper Ben Foster says about the way he became aware of his own thinking (inner self-talk) and its impact on his levels of inner confidence.

"Confidence is the difference. In the early stages of my career, I had a great build, a great frame, but I didn't have the confidence. If you haven't got the other element – the mental side – you can't succeed. You won't succeed. If you go into a game thinking, don't make a mistake, don't mess up, it's inevitable that you will. That's what my Psychologist gave me. I basically went into games thinking I'm going to save everything they throw at me today. I'm much better than these attempts on my goal. If players can get work with a psychologist, it makes the world of difference."

When reading the above, notice how Ben shifted his inner self-talk from negative to positive, and the subsequent impact it had on his game. Building a positive inner dialogue or internal voice is so important for players and coaches. When doubt is the enemy of belief, the voice that fuels hope in moments of despair or despondency is a vital element that can be the difference. Have a look at some of the positive and empowering statements elite athletes and coaches have used in the past.

- "I CAN respond to any challenge in the game because I have the ability."
- "I AM in complete control of my performance."
- "I AM confident in myself to compete against any opponent."
- "I BELIEVE I deserve every opportunity I get."
- "I BELIEVE I attract great things into my life."
- "I WILL never EVER give up."

As you read through these statements, I'm sure you feel a positive shift in your emotional energy, particularly if you believe in them or feel a significant connection.

When you reinforce positive empowering thoughts through self-talk that inspire and boost self-belief, you build the mental muscles required to succeed by fuelling a level of focused optimism.

As a coach, you can encourage your players to use self-talk in three simple steps:

Frame thoughts

When describing critical moments for players (like responding to a mistake) you can suggest a way to think in response to adversity. "If it doesn't quite work, or you make a mistake, just think to yourself 'I'll get the next one right' or 'I will improve this'." In offering players these options, you help them to replace their own negative thoughts after mistakes with positive empowering ones so that they don't get stuck in a negative downward spiral.

Know the script

You can ask players to come up with their own self-talk scripts that empower and energise them. For example, writing down a personal phrase – such as "Effort is everything" – in the dressing room and pinning it inside their locker door is a way to help players repeat empowering self-talk over and over again.

Practice makes progress

On the practice pitch, out on the grass, you can walk through specific scenarios that players will face during a match. When painting the matchday picture, you can instruct the players, "This is how I want you to think from an attacking set play. Think quick, play quick." Coaching mantras are simple, clear, and concise ways to trigger inner self-talk for players during key matchday moments.

Physiology and Body Language

Research has shown that consciously changing your body language can alter your mood significantly. Standing confidently tall, strong, and steady heightens psychological focus and prepares the body to perform.

In 2010, Social Psychologist Amy Cuddy, the speaker of the second most-watched TED talk of all time, detailed empirical findings associated with what is now known as the 'power pose'.

Amy found that when people are asked to pose in powerful positions (think of Superman, hands on hips, head up, chest out), they produce higher levels of testosterone and lower levels of the stress hormone cortisol. Increased testosterone helps ready a player for the challenge prior to facing the opposition; it is the body's way of hormonally preparing for events to come.

Testosterone levels also increase before we engage in competition and after a win, but fall after a defeat. Thus, by stimulating testosterone production, power poses can reinforce dominance before and after competition. By contrast, weaker body language poses of a more submissive nature elicit adverse effects in people, lowering testosterone levels and heightening the stress hormone cortisol. They also induce a sense of anxiety and apprehension.

To the hormonal and emotional systems, it appears that body language can be a defining element of thinking and feeling like a winner.

As a coach, you can use body language to help your players by:

Modelling positive empowering body language yourself

When you stand tall, walk with strength, and hold your head up high, players will respond. They will start to mirror and model your example and put it into practice themselves.

Tell, See, Do

Pick the key moment to *instruct* your players before competition to 'be strong, walk tall, and hold your heads up high'. Say it, mean it, and do it yourself. This will act to create a positive atmosphere and positively prepare body and mind.

Role Model Memory

Ask the players to think of their favourite, most confident, and successful player. Ask them to imagine how they feel right before they go out and perform. Ask them to picture how they walk out onto the pitch and stand right before they play. Ask them to think of a time when they've seen their favourite player succeed in looking confident. How did they look, stand, and walk? Tell them to notice how confident and strong they are.

Try it on

Set up an opportunity for your players to practice their own power poses and walks. It's important that this is authentic, real, and not forced. If it's their first time, then it may feel new and unfamiliar at the start, but when players model positive physiology and focus their attention on walking as their most confident selves, it can become a very important part of their pre-match preparation.

Breathing

The power of breathing, and its impact on the mental and emotional states we enter into, is vastly underestimated. Through breathing consciously, becoming aware of our breath, and focusing on rhythm and depth – an individual can bring about powerful changes in him- or herself. When we inhale, and expand our lungs full of fresh oxygen, physiological and psychological changes take place. Breathing influences the body and the mind and can have positive lasting effects for reducing anxiety, stress, and depression.

Medical research designed to assess the positive impact and influence of 'conscious breathing' has illustrated its benefits to health and wellbeing. Becoming consciously aware of your breathing can act to centre your attention, bring calm and focus to thinking, and relax muscles – all of which are conducive to feeling happier, healthier, and more fulfilled. As we've discovered in previous chapters, a happier healthier person leads to the creation of a better player.

Exercises

Here are some simple breathing exercises that both players and coaches can use.

Find a quiet place where you will be undisturbed. Sit comfortably in a straight-backed chair and place your feet flat on the floor. With your eyes open or closed take a deep breath in, filling your lungs with air. Exhale slowly whilst at the same time counting down from 5 to 1.

Practise getting to 1 at the same time as you fully exhale.

Repeat this for as long as you can, focusing your attention on the rising and falling of your sternum, stomach, and chest area. During this exercise, move your attention from one body part to another, becoming aware of how relaxed and calm each body part feels before moving on to the next. If you feel yourself becoming distracted at any stage, slowly bring your attention back to the air coming in and out of your mouth, filling your lungs with air. Repeat this exercise for at least 10 minutes a day.

By becoming consciously aware of your breathing, you will simultaneously strengthen your potential to be more focused, less distracted, and gain more control over your mental and physical state.

The Mind Sweep

This breathing exercise is designed to clear one's mind: sharpening one's focus and blocking out distraction. It's perfect for centring attention and bringing oneself completely into the moment, feeling more energised and engaged with the task at hand.

Take a deep breath in through your nose, inhaling fully, before exhaling with one quick sharp breath out, freeing the air from your lungs completely.

Slowly raise your shoulders to your ears during the inhalation phase to match the speed of your breathing and allow them to drop straight back down during the quick exhalation phase.

Repeat this exercise just before engaging with an important task for best results.

As always, a combination of breathing, self-talk, and powerful body language or physiology can improve mental and emotional states immediately. Pay attention to the way each exercise feels to you and adapt where necessary to gain maximum results. Imagine that these exercises are like trying on an outfit in a shop. Feel free to try them on and play with them to find the ones that fit best; the ones that offer the best combination.

A coach's final message

A first-team coach once told me that he wanted his players to walk out onto the pitch with three simple things in their minds.

1. We are ready.
2. I am confident in you.
3. Enjoy Yourself.

What is the last thing you want your players to think when they walk out onto the pitch? What is your final message?

The Pre-Performance Routine

> **What we think, we become.**
> Buddha

Elite athletes, coaches, and managers ignite the unconquerable warrior within themselves to be at their best when it matters most. Although they might do this in different ways, what is certain is that they make the switch from 'real self' to 'performer self' and put on their game faces. They get themselves ready to enter competition with strength, confidence, and complete self-belief.

One of the ways to become an effective performer is by preparing the mind before actual performance.

Pre-performance routines are a fantastic way to set a structure on a team's performance, get clarity, focus minds, and centre people's attention. Pre-performance routines can help teams shift from negative to positive, from distracted to focused, and from anxious to supremely confident.

Although coaches develop and deliver pre-performance routines to their teams, they can also use pre-performance routines themselves. It's important to note here that pre-performance routines are not the same as superstitions. Pre-performance routines are specific behaviours that lead to specific performance improvements. Visualising a confident tackle, or the arc of a cross – as a player – is not the same thing as putting your left sock on last in the dressing room. Superstitions do, without doubt, have some power for some people but, for now, let's focus on the specific and defined processes that assist teams in training or competition.

Using this specialised mental training technique, team members will be able to:

- Practice techniques mentally and physically before performance.
- Gain clarity and structure to thinking.
- Feel more prepared emotionally, and ready to compete.
- Connect central nervous systems to positive physiology.
- Boost self-belief, concentration, and composure under pressure.

PRINCIPLE 9

Here are some examples of pre-performance routines that athletes and coaches can use at their performance edges.

- Visualise perfect performance by seeing – in your mind's eye – each action and contribution as perfectly executed as it could be.
- Physically anchor and run through critical movements, positions, and techniques. Actively move through the moments ahead, seeing, thinking, and feeling good about the image in your mind.
- Create positive empowerment with a strong, confident inner dialogue, affirming over and over again the success and achievement within reach. *"I will succeed. I can do this."*
- Breathe in the positive expectations you hold for yourself, adopting power poses and centring your attention on power, strength, speed, confidence, light, energy, and positivity.
- Bounce to inspired music playlists that make you feel good and which stir up positive emotion.
- Recall successful past experiences in your mind and know that it is within you to be successful again.
- In your mind, go over (and over again) the positive beliefs you hold about yourself.
- Go to the mirror, and tell yourself about these key strengths.
- In private environments such as the home and car, pin up trigger cards containing energy words that you can relate to in the dressing room. Reflect on these in the final minutes leading up to performance.
- Pray to the God you believe in, if you believe in one.
- Watch the key positive highlights of previous performances on TVs or phones or tablets and see your successful self in action.
- Tense and relax your muscles to release tension; channel your energy in the final seconds before competition.
- Run your eyes over the key roles and responsibilities you have to produce to become clear and confident.

Image and Appearance

How do you want to be seen?

Your image must reflect the message you want to convey. A club tracksuit and trainers with a cup of tea and a newspaper under your arm may be the relaxed tone you wish to set. A suit and a tie followed by a team meeting over PowerPoint may be the professional tone you need to inject. Whatever you believe is needed, make sure your appearance reflects your intention.

Your communication, tone, and speed and rhythm of speech in the changing room is critical. There's no need to bombard the players with last-minute information. That's what training has been for across the week. You are now fully prepared and, as coach, you are there to infuse your players with confidence, clarity, and calm. If you want your players to start fast, speed up your rhythm of speech; if you feel you need to help them relax, speak slowly and quietly. As coach, you must be the example for staff and players.

Some coaches make a cup of tea and go for a walk for a few minutes to run through, in their own minds, what it is they want to say and achieve in their team talk. Others speak to their staff privately before setting up in the changing rooms to ensure they are clear and are able to pass on any observations or important pieces of information. Through taking control of your routine, you give yourself the best possible chance to achieve a consistent approach; as such, by the time you speak with the players, you are clear, confident, and consciously aware of the message you want to deliver.

Knowing which player to speak to, and which ones to leave alone, is also important. Each individual prepares differently before the game. Every one of them is unique.

> As a player I didn't like the coaches speaking to me that much in the dressing room before the game; I wanted to prepare in my own time and space. Now, as a coach, I'm aware of how I used to feel before the game, and I ask myself the same question about our players. I've got to learn which ones like to be spoken to, and which ones don't, because they're all different.
>
> Steven Reid – Premier League First Team Coach

Knowing when not to speak is as important as knowing when to. For example, following a tough game and a narrow loss, Brentford boss Dean Smith said one sentence in the dressing room after the game,

"Let's get showered, we'll talk about it tomorrow." He knew that the players needed their own time and space to process the result and the emotion. He also knew himself well. He didn't want to say something until he had also reflected properly. That's what clever coaches do; they use emotional intelligence to read the context of the situation and decide a course of action.

'How do we become successful?' - The 10 Key Components

After working with an elite coach on a senior men's soccer team in England, we decided to devise a simple but effective affirmation to put up in the players' changing room.

The 10 key components of this team's winning approach were founded after a workshop which was devised to answer the question 'how do we become successful?'

This list isn't a secret recipe for success; it was the team's unique way of expressing what they felt *their* roadmap to success was. It ended up aiding matchday preparation, with core principles that would guide their endeavours together. Both players and staff contributed, were connected to a collective common understanding, and held themselves and each other accountable.

Here are the 10 key components they agreed on together:

1. Come back to self – Look in the mirror

I promise myself to be so dedicated to my own self-improvement that I have no time to criticise others.

2. Stop making excuses – Avoid a blame culture

Take ownership for winning, losing, successes, and failures.

3. Commit to action

Do something every day to be better; connect intention to action.

4. Clarity builds confidence and consistency

Be sure of what it is that you want. Be sure of how you are going to get it.

5. Honestly reflect on constant and never-ending improvement

Great performers always ask how they can make things better, faster.

6. Build the Response-ABLE mindset

The setbacks, the difficulty, the challenges, the failures; they do not determine your destiny. Your response to those times, people and circumstances do. It's your decisions – not your conditions – that determine your results.

7. Connect to your reason why

The single most empowering motivation. Know your purpose. Get meaning. Know your reason why.

8. Fun! Excitement ignites the flames

We all smile in the same language! Keep it enjoyable!

9. Get a thinking partner and share ideas

We all need a little help from our friends, and we also need honest constructive criticism with a solution in mind. Share experiences to help you think through the performances.

10. Never, never, never give up

No matter what. No matter how tough things get. Tough times don't last. Tough people do.

Specific actions: During the match

During the match, the majority of players I have spoken with are so focused on the game that they are largely unaware of what the coach is saying or doing. In the professional game, the noise within the stadium makes it near impossible for the players to hear anything from their coach on the sideline; especially if they are 100 yards away on the opposite side of the pitch. That's why, as a coach, stepping outside of the action can be useful to 'check in' with what's really happening in the game. Here's how a Premier League coach from West Bromwich Albion FC retained focus during the game.

What's the bigger picture?

Check the opposition's formation and personnel in the first five minutes, and at regular intervals throughout the game – is it what you expected? Is there anything that needs to change?

Use the eye in the sky

Check in with the analysts, if you have them, who can see the structure and shape of the formation.

Control the clock

Are we on task with our match's time-specific goals? First 15 minutes, 10 minutes to go?

Tactical plays

What are the hot moments? Counter presses ... triggers to go tight ... signals from set-pieces ... game plan adjustments?

Personnel

Who needs encouragement? Who needs a kick up the arse? Who needs a little more instruction?

In finding your own structure for a matchday management process, you will be able to regain perspective during the heat of the moment. Regain your perspective and stay focused.

Half-Time

> **The last thing they hear is probably the only thing they remember.**
>
> Glenn Hoddle

Whilst much has been said, written, and recommended about half-time team talks, it is important at this stage to recall a central theme of this book. In essence, the future coach is a coach who places the needs of their players at the centre of proceedings.

A key question to ask before delivering any half-time team talk is *what do the players need right now?* Each situation will be different, whether winning or losing, playing well or not performing.

One of the best half-time case studies I have ever researched was the 2005 Champions League final, hosted in Istanbul, between Liverpool and AC Milan. In what must go down as one of the most inspired comebacks in football history, Liverpool saw themselves 0-3 down to a rampant Milan side. Thoroughly outplayed in the first half, Liverpool's coach at the time – Rafa Benitez – had a challenging task ahead. After making some tactical changes and setting a simple goal of winning the second half, he allowed his captain – Steven Gerrard – to speak and have the final word with the team.

As the players anticipated what their skipper would say, he stood up and walked over to the dressing room door to hold it open. The sound of 17,000 Liverpool fans singing at the top of their voices came rushing in through the tunnel. "You'll never walk alone, walk on, walk on with hope in your hearts." Gerrard turned to the team and said, "If they still believe, then so do we, now come on."

Not only did his spoken leadership inspire the team in a defining moment, he scored Liverpool's first goal, played a part in the second, and won the penalty for the third. Critically, Rafa Benitez knew the power he had in his captain at half-time. He knew what the players needed most. He understood that after selling his game plan, leadership was going to be the defining factor.

Milan's coach – Carlo Ancelotti – on the other hand, faced an over-confident and complacent Milan dressing room at half-time. Crucially, his players believed that the match was already won. In fact, some were applauding the crowd and taking pictures with fans. Ancelotti's task was to prevent them from going out for the second half thinking the contest was already over. Both dressing rooms had their relative challenges at half-time. Both required their coaches to deliver in the *context* of the competition. Both needed their coaches to place their needs at the centre of proceedings. Only one succeeded.

At half-time, emotions can run high. More often though, after allowing a period for rest and recuperation, it is a key opportunity for the coach to communicate with absolute clarity.

At half-time, as the coach, you must prioritise your key messages to maximise your impact and influence, and do so practically. Following a pattern that players become sub-consciously used to, can act as a platform for security. A safe-house regardless of the situation. An anchor in the storm of adversity, or a grounded place during success. Providing a routine will pay dividends: rest, video clip/whiteboard, last word and out. Whatever you believe is the most important routine for your players offers certainty in an uncertain world of competition.

Specific Actions

Provide an opportunity for players to become self-aware, and focus on the prioritised challenges at hand.

Allow players the chance to share their thoughts. How do they *think* and *feel* at half-time?

Provide clear solutions to the problems thus helping the players to reduce anxiety and negative stress.

Encourage individuals and sell the game plan. Motivate through strategy. Have a plan, but be flexible.

Focus on CAN. Be positive. Boost spirits and players' self-belief.

Summary

Managing matchday is, in reality, about managing yourself.

Your thoughts, feelings, and behaviour are the guiding signposts for the entire team – both players and staff. Making sure that you are positive, focused, and full of energy are crucial ingredients required to help your players do the same.

Ensure you surround yourself with people who will share your ideas and tackle challenges head-on. Take the advice of trusted mentors and thinking partners who will help you think outside of your own mind. Surround yourself with intelligent people who are willing to help.

As coach, you can't cover every base every time, so it's important you encourage others to work and support you, allowing you to focus your efforts on your central priorities.

Know your players well and see the world through their eyes. Practise the habit of personal reflection which will build self-awareness and allow you to improve your capacity to adapt positively.

Above all else, place the players' needs in the centre of the equation: *what do they need, right now, the most?*

WARRIORS NEVER GIVE UP

The following letter was given to a group of players from their coach at St. Kevin's football club in Dublin, Ireland. Ahead of four national youth team cup finals in the Academy, coach Alan Caffrey found a speech given by General Patton, delivered to the United States Third Army. It has gone down as one of the most effective and inspirational speeches ever delivered to a team. Alan Caffrey believed that the speech encompassed all his players needed, to be the best every day, and to help them live a better life.

Today you must do more than is required. Never think that you have done enough or that your job is finished; there's always something that can be done to help ensure victory. You can't let others be responsible for getting you started. You must be a self-starter. You must possess that spark of individual initiative that sets the leaders apart from the rest. Motivation is the key to being one step ahead of everyone else and standing head and shoulders above the crowd. Once you get going, don't stop. Always be on the lookout for the chance to do something better. Never stop trying. Fill yourself with the warrior's spirit and send that warrior into action.

I want you to read this in times of self-doubt to reinforce that people may question your talent but they will never question your heart and desire to be better than you were yesterday. The rewards you will receive will be priceless. The joy and satisfaction of your achievements will live with you for the rest of your life. Start now and start to fulfil your dreams.

After the final training session before the finals, the four teams trained together. At the end of the session, Alan called the de-brief. Recognising that the players were becoming anxious about being club record breakers, he told them not to worry about all the talk of winning the four finals. He told each team that they could only win one final, the final that they played in. It was up to the other teams to win their own finals. He could see the pressure on the players' shoulders lift straight away. Then he told them that he had a letter for them – just for players NOT parents. He told them to read it that night and just before they left for the finals.

Three weeks later, he got a visit from one of the parents who said that he read his son's letter whilst he was asleep. The father told the coach how he was moved by the letter. After the final, the player's father told his son not to worry about the winner's medal. He advised him instead to keep the letter for the rest of his life, as its value was much, much more. It just so happened that St. Kevin's FC did win each final, and created record-breaking history for the club.

EPILOGUE

Writing this book has been a highly challenging and rewarding process. As we have seen, from studying biographical histories and the great coaches of the past, a pre-requisite for sustained coaching success is the ability to keep learning. One of the best pieces of advice offered to me by my previous youth team manager, Eddie Howe, was "You never stop learning." In a sense, this simple piece of advice has formed the very nature of this book. The lessons shared have been pieced together with the intention of helping coaches to get curious about their practices, behaviour, and philosophies. By exploring some of the practical principles covered, it is my hope that the 'art' of coaching has been presented in equal importance to the science. We may not be able to predict the future – but we can create a better one for our players if we're able to see through their eyes and feel with their hearts.

Although entitled *The Future Coach*, the lasting principles of coaching success are, of course, timeless, although the structure and delivery of them in the modern day soccer climate may change. For example, a coach may agree that *communication* is a central component of success. Modes of communication are *changing* with societal shifts and technological advances. These changes influence *how* and *when* messages are delivered. Previously, coaches may have held open discussions or lengthy team meetings to communicate with their players; today, faster modes of alternative communication are available. Nowadays, many players instantly access their match footage and player de-briefs online through video analysis and statistical data via a handheld device. The way people learn, today, is different to 10 years ago, which means that we, as coaches, must adapt the way we teach. Innovation has become a central tenet of future success. It is for this reason that the great teachers of the past remain consistently able to influence their present coaching environments positively and thus attain future success.

Creating the time and space to 'think' as a coach can be a challenge in itself. However, in order to grow, learn, and improve – thinking, reflecting, and considering your coaching practice and principles are fundamental to advancing your development journey.

The dawn of a new era for modern-day coaching and leadership is upon us. This will mean that the very nature of future success will depend on a coach's capacity to think forwards and remain ahead of the game. The constant fast-paced and ever-changing multi-dimensional landscape of coaching creates new challenges for coaches to succeed. Creating more emotionally intelligent, independent players of tomorrow requires

EPILOGUE

coaches to learn and apply new skills today. I hope that this book has, in some part, helped you as a coach on your journey to do just that.

Deliberate Soccer Practice: 50 Small-Sided Football Games to Improve Decision-Making

by Ray Power

Small-sided games are the epicentre of soccer improvement. Done right, they can play a huge role in the development of players. The environment created through these games makes it possible not just to 'let the game be the teacher,' but also to improve specific skills and tactics – all in the context of the real game.

Aimed at football coaches of all levels, but with a particular emphasis on coaches who work with youth players, 50 Small-Sided Football Games to Improve Decision-Making is comprised of 50 practices, and carefully designed to be adaptable to suit the needs of the players you work with.

Book number four in Ray Power's "Deliberate Soccer Practice" series, the exercises will challenge players and give them real-world decisions to make. Sections include: Possession-Based Small-Sided Games (SSGs), SSGs for Attacking and Finishing, SSGs for Defending, SSGs for Goalkeepers, SSGs for Transitions and Restarts, and Other Varieties of SSG.

Other titles in the series: Deliberate Soccer Practice: 50 Attacking Exercises to Improve Decision-Making | Deliberate Soccer Practice: 50 Defending Football Exercises to Improve Decision-Making | Deliberate Soccer Practice: 50 Passing & Possession Football Exercises to Improve Decision-Making

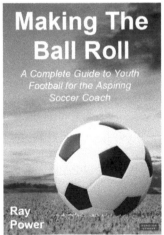

Ray Power is also the author of the internationally acclaimed book **Making The Ball Roll: A Complete Guide to Youth Football for the Aspiring Soccer Coach**

Play Like Pep Guardiola's Barcelona: A Soccer Coach's Guide

Written by Agustín Peraita, FCBEscola Project Director at Sao Paulo FC Barcelona, this book is for soccer coaches looking to understand and implement Pep Guardiola's tactical approach and coaching methodology for that 2009-2010 Barça side. Containing more than 50 illustrations, detailing on-field drills, Principles / Subprinciples / Sub-SubPrinciples, tactical diagrams and weekly planning schedules, this practical and to-the-point book focuses explicitly on the preseason period as it lays the foundation for how a team will train, play, and perform over the season. Indeed, regular season training is simply a continuation of everything a team learns and implements during this phase, based on the playing schedule and other resources at a coach's disposal. The playing philosophy, model of play, associated drills, and weekly training schedule are implemented from day one that the squad assembles.

"Play Like Pep Guardiola's Barcelona: A Soccer Coach's Guide" provides a theoretical base alongside practical guidance for coaches (even if they do not have elite players such as Lionel Messi, Xavi, and Andrés Iniesta) to develop the 'play' that Guardiola developed during his second season at Barça. Incorporating detailed discussion of the Model of Play, Tactical Periodization, the four phases of the game, positional play, and more, a methodological framework is presented that can be used to train almost any proficient football team whether amateur, semi-professional or professional.

WINNING YOUR PLAYERS
THROUGH TRUST, LOYALTY, AND RESPECT

DeAngelo Wiser

Winning Your Players through Trust, Loyalty, and Respect: A Soccer Coach's Guide by DeAngelo Wiser

In order to develop the best soccer players, who can achieve their very best in the game, a coach needs to instill three central qualities: Trust, Loyalty, and Respect. Without them, your words have no meaning and lack the power to inspire your players to reach new heights; with them, your team gains the ability and motivation to over-achieve.

Coach DeAngelo Wiser is a soccer coach with more than 20 years' experience of working with high school players, during which time he has gathered District and Regional Titles, and Coach of the Year honors. In Winning Your Players, he offers accumulated wisdom, insight, and solutions garnered from years of developing players and working with them in competitive environments at key moments. His methods of building Trust, Loyalty, and Respect, give every coach the ability to have a positive impact in practice, the game, and – more importantly – in life.

BUILDING A SUCCESSFUL HIGH SCHOOL SPORTS PROGRAM

DeAngelo Wiser

Knowing the best way to navigate and deal with challenges is the key to relating to your players. Wiser's emphasis on the role of decision making through consistency, character, and integrity are what makes this book essential in every coach's career.

DeAngelo Wiser is also the author of **Building a Successful High School Sports Program**

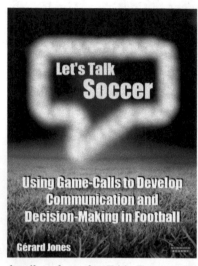

Let's Talk Soccer: Using Game-Calls to Develop Communication and Decision-Making in Football by Gérard Jones

Soccer coaches across all levels of the game share a common and simple dilemma: how best to improve their players. One of the best ways to do this is through improved communication and how we individualize our messages to our players. It's fundamentally important for coaches to provide quality communication with clear detail and, as the FA's Future Game Philosophy makes clear, "Mastery of innovative coaching methods that utilize communication styles is the mark of a gifted coach, and will be an essential requirement for the game of the future."

Examples of good communications that develop game understanding and skill are seen with elite football coaches such as Jose Mourinho and Pep Guardiola. Their messages are directly linked to how they want their teams to play, hence the importance of having a coaching vocabulary that players can understand.

Let's Talk Soccer introduces 'Game-calls', game-specific communication designed to enhance decision making and skill among players. Through Game-calls your team will become more organized, and your players will understand – as individuals – how to play within your playing philosophy.

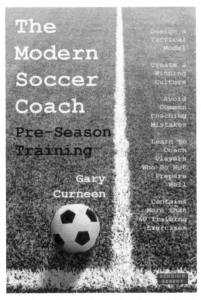

The Modern Soccer Coach: Pre-Season Training by Gary Curneen

When it comes to building successful soccer teams, pre-season is a critical time. It's the perfect time for the coach to create a team identity, set standards, develop effective training habits, and reinforce winning behaviors. Get it right and you can set the foundation required to catapult your team towards an excellent season. Get it wrong, however, and your season might never recover.

This book looks at how pre-season has changed over the past 10 years, and offers ways for coaches to adapt their work and methods to deal with these changes accordingly. Pre-season is about much more than fitness testing, long-distance running, and grueling physical work. "The Modern Soccer Coach – Pre-Season Training" looks at new, innovative ways to engage players so that they want to train at the maximum every day, and push towards new limits for the new season ahead.

Aimed at soccer coaches of all levels who work with players of all age groups, this book focuses on maximizing every minute you have with your team to help them prepare to set the highest of standards for the season ahead. The book offers a unique insight into how the best coaches in the world are preparing their teams from day one.

With over 60 training exercises designed specifically to challenge your players to their maximum physically, technically, tactically, and mentally, this is pre-season training like you have never seen it before.

Other titles from Gary Curneen include:

The Modern Soccer Coach 2014: A Four Dimensional Approach

The Modern Soccer Coach: Position-Specific Training

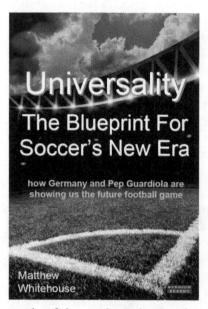

Universality | The Blueprint for Soccer's New Era: How Germany and Pep Guardiola are showing us the Future Football Game by Matthew Whitehouse

The game of soccer is constantly in flux; new ideas, philosophies and tactics mould the present and shape the future.

Since the turn of the century we have witnessed dramatic changes in the beautiful game: new types of player, new coaching methods and tactical innovations have all enhanced and changed the sport of football. The technical, tactical, physical and psychological skills needs of the modern player – from the goalkeeper to centre forward – have all been enhanced. In a nutshell, the modern game is quicker as well as being technically and tactically more advanced than for previous generations. Excitingly, the future promises to be even faster, more technical, and more demanding of its players!

In this book, Matthew Whitehouse – acclaimed author of **The Way Forward: Solutions to England's Football Failings** – looks in-depth at the past decade of the game, taking the reader on a journey into football's evolution. Examining the key changes that have occurred since the turn of the century, right up to the present, the book looks at the evolution of tactics, coaching, position-specific play and -of course – Pep Guardiola. They have led us to this moment: to the rise of universality.

Soccer Brain: The 4C Coaching Model for Developing World Class Player Mindsets and a Winning Football Team by Dan Abrahams

Coaching soccer is demanding. Impossible to perfect, it requires a broad knowledge of many performance areas including technique, tactics, psychology and the social aspects of human development. The first two components are covered in detail in many texts – but Soccer Brain uniquely offers a comprehensive guide to developing the latter two – player mindsets and winning teams.

The environment that a coach creates, and the relationships formed with players, is the bedrock of performance and achievement. Coaches who are able to deliver students of the game, and who are able to help players execute skills and tactics under pressure are the future leaders of the world's most loved sport. Soccer Brain teaches coaches to train players to compete with confidence, with commitment, with intelligence, and as part of a team. The positive messages from each chapter of Soccer Brain help coaches to develop players through patience, repetition, reinforcement, re-appraisal and high value relationships.

Dan Abrahams is also the author of

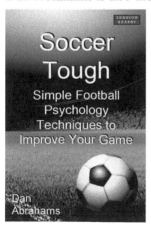

Soccer Tough: Simple Football Psychology Techniques to Improve Your Game

Soccer Tough 2: Advanced Psychology Techniques for Footballers

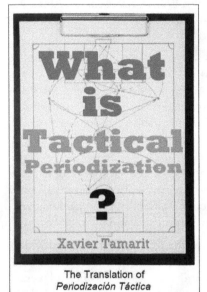

The Translation of
Periodización Táctica

What is Tactical Periodization? By Xavier Tamarit

Originally developed by Vitór Frade, at the University of Porto, Tactical Periodization is a methodology – popularized by coaches such as José Mourinho and Andre Villas Boas – that trains soccer players through a logical process that focuses on four moments of the game.

These four moments are: Offensive Organisation, the Transition from Defence to Attack, Defensive Organisation, and the Transition from Attack to Defence. Through Tactical Periodization, the aim is to develop players to rapidly alter their on-field behaviours according to the tactical context of the match, and what actually unfolds in front of them. In turn, every training exercise focuses on at least one of the four moments, and always the coach's tactical game model of how he wants his team to play. In doing so, football players prepare and learn how best to conquer the often unpredictable matches that they encounter competitively.

This book is the English language translation of the acclaimed book *Periodización Táctica* by world-renowned coach and sports science specialist Xavier Tamarit.

CPSIA information can be obtained
at www.ICGtesting.com
Printed in the USA
LVHW05s0956280918
591595LV00021BA/380/P

9 781911 121435